PAUL'S
Prison Letters

Daniel J. Harrington

PAUL'S
Prison Letters

**Spiritual Commentaries
on Paul's Letters to Philemon,
the Philippians, and the Colossians**

New City Press

Published in the United States by New City Press
202 Cardinal Rd., Hyde Park, NY 12538
©1997 Daniel J. Harrington

Cover design by Nick Cianfarani
Cover art: The Conversion of Paul by Russell Goodman. Found in St. Peter's
Lutheran Church in Ottawa, Ontario.

Library of Congress Cataloging-in-Publication Data:

Harrington, Daniel J.
    Paul's prison letters : spiritual commentaries on Paul's letters to Philemon,
  the Philippians, and the Colossians / by Daniel J. Harrington.
        p.   cm. — (Spiritual commentaries)
    Includes bibliographical references.
    ISBN 1-56548-088-0
    1. Bible.   N.T.   Philemon—Commentaries.   2. Bible.   N.T.
  Philippians—Commentaries.   3. Bible.   N.T.   Colossians-
  -Commentaries.   4. Bible.   N.T.   Philemon—Devotional use.
  5. Bible.   N.T.   Philippians—Devotional use.   6. Bible.   N.T.
  Colossians—Devotional use.   I. Title.   II. Series.
BS2765.3.H37   1997
227'.6077—dc21   96-46245

Printed in the United States of America

Contents

Prologue

This volume presents "spiritual commentaries" on three Pauline letters: Philemon, Philippians, and Colossians. For each letter there is an introduction, the text according to the New American Bible (revised edition, 1988) with an exposition for each passage, and reflections on the letter's significance for Christian life today. The commentaries seek to open up for non-specialists the spiritual riches contained in these texts and to help people today to make them part of their Christian spirituality.

Besides explaining the meaning of these texts, I want to illustrate a method of studying biblical texts and of using them as helps toward progress in the spiritual life. I want to show how the basic concerns of biblical exegesis (literary analysis, history, theology) can lead naturally into personal appropriation in meditation, prayer, and action.

In many ways this book, although different in scope, is a companion to *How To Read the Gospels—Answers to Common Questions* (New City Press, 1996). Chapters 3 and 5 of that book contain explanations and illustrations of how one should go about reading Gospel texts. As I was writing it, I felt the desire to write another book that would introduce ordinary folk to Paul and his letters, and would at the same time give an initiation to methods for reading Paul's letters both intelligently and reverently. I am grateful to New City Press for the opportunity to make this wish a reality.

Introduction to Paul's
Letters from Prison

The three letters treated in this volume—to Philemon, to the Philippians, and to the Colossians—portray Paul as a prisoner (see also 2 Tm 2:9 and Eph 4:1).

These three prison letters are not as famous as other Pauline letters are. The earliest Pauline letter is 1 Thessalonians, which is important as a witness to the rich theological vocabulary that had developed in the twenty years between Jesus' death in A.D. 30 and the letter's composition in A.D. 51. Paul's letter to the Galatians provides information about Paul's life in Judaism and his call to Christian faith and apostleship to the Gentiles. It also gives a sophisticated biblical argument to prove that Gentile Christians were not obligated to become Jews and observe the Jewish Law.

The two letters to the Corinthians are lengthy and full of information about Paul's efforts to give guidance to a troubled community that he had founded. The letter to the Romans is undoubtedly the best known and theologically most rich among the Pauline letters. In it Paul describes the revelation of God's righteousness in Christ: Why we needed it, what it has done for us, where it fits in the history of salvation, and what difference it should make in Christian life.

The three Pauline letters treated in this volume might not match those other letters in historical significance or length. Nevertheless, they can provide a good starting point for studying and appreciating the whole corpus of Paul's letters.

Paul's letters are not easy to read. This is acknowledged even in the New Testament: "In them there are some things hard to understand" (2 Pt 3:16). Paul's letter to Philemon can serve as a good introduction because it is short (only 25 verses) and follows the basic outline adopted in the other Pauline letters: greeting, thanksgiving and prayer, body, travel plans, and farewells. It can help the beginner to understand the literary conventions that governed the composition of all the Pauline letters.

Most of Paul's letters were written to communities that he had founded. They were one way of his continuing to give encouragement and advice even in his physical absence. Paul's letter to the Philippians allows us to glimpse his very personal relationship with what some have called his favorite community. We can participate in his joys and frustrations through the letter. In fact, it may well be a collection of three letters written by Paul to the Philippians over a fairly short period of time (2 Corinthians may also be a compilation of several letters.) If this is so, we can then chart the twists and turns in Paul's pastoral relationship with his favorite community. We can see what problems arose, the different facets of Paul's personality, and what advice he gave at different points.

The letter to the Colossians has many links with the letters to Philemon and to the Philippians. And yet in its language and theological concepts it differs from them and from the other letters definitely written by Paul (1 Thessalonians, Galatians, 1 and 2 Corinthians, Romans). Many scholars regard (correctly, I think) Colossians as written not directly by Paul but by a co-worker or an admirer to confront a situation that had arisen in and around Colossae about A.D. 80, some twenty years after Paul's death. Study of the letter to the Colossians can alert us to the phenomenon of "pseudepigraphy" in the collection of Pauline letters. Other letters that may have been composed in Paul's name are 2 Thessalonians, Ephesians, 1 and 2 Timothy, and Titus.

All these issues—the form of the Pauline letter (Philemon), Paul's personal relations with the addressees and the possibility of a collection of letters (Philippians), and the convention of pseudepigraphy (Colossians)— show why these prison letters can serve as a good introduction to the Pauline writings as a whole.

Paul in Prison

That Paul was arrested in Jerusalem and imprisoned first at Caesarea Maritima ("by the sea") in Palestine and then in Rome is clear from Acts 21–28. If the prison letters were composed in either of those places, they would have to be dated late in Paul's career—in the late 50s or early 60s of the first century A.D. But the chief problem with those places is that the letters refer to many messengers and visits between Paul, his co-workers, and the recipients.

An earlier imprisonment at Ephesus, though not directly mentioned in the New Testament, would better explain the situations presupposed in the letters. Ephesus was a major city for Paul's activity during his life and probably the place of the Pauline "school" after his death.

He wrote Galatians and 1 and 2 Corinthians from Ephesus. In 2 Corinthians (see 1:8-11; 11:23) he alludes to imprisonments that may have occurred at Ephesus. If Paul wrote these letters from prison at Ephesus, he most likely did so in the mid-50s of the first century.

Paul gives few details about his imprisonment. He was far more interested in the apostolic mission that he continued to direct from prison. From the letters to Philemon (see 19, 22) and to the Philippians (see 1:12-26) one gets the impression that Paul is awaiting trial and that he is hopeful to be released and be able to travel and to visit his friends.

The precise reason for Paul's imprisonment is not clear from the letters. Paul contends that he is suffering for the sake of the gospel of Jesus Christ and rejoices that even his imprisonment is contributing to the spreading of the gospel (see Phil 1:12-18). From Acts we get the impression that Paul's arrival in a city was disruptive both to the local Jewish community and to the local businessmen. These groups in turn put pressure on the Roman imperial administrators to do something about Paul.

The precise conditions of Paul's imprisonment are nowhere described. We know that conditions in Roman jails could be very harsh. Many prisoners had to wear chains that severely restricted their movements. Indeed, the Greek word for "chain" (*desmos*) is the basis for the term for prisoner (*desmios* = one who wears a chain)—the term that Paul uses to describe his own situation. Nevertheless, Paul's letters from prison indicate that he could have visitors (his co-workers), could take advantage of the services of a slave (Onesimus), and could receive reports and write letters.

Being a prisoner gave Paul a certain moral authority. Having brought many of those addressed to Christian faith, Paul could point to his imprisonment for the sake of the gospel as proof of his authenticity as an apostle of Christ Jesus, and thus put pressure on his readers to do the right thing and to avoid perversions of his gospel.

Reading and Praying Paul's Letters from Prison

The three letters discussed in this book are part of the Christian New Testament and as such are Holy Scripture. When read in a liturgical setting they are called the "word of God." These texts can serve as a good introduction not only to Paul and his letters but also to reading biblical texts with reason and reverence.

The systematic analysis of biblical texts is called exegesis. The basic aim of exegesis is to explain the meaning of the biblical text in its historical setting and with attention to its theological significance.

For each of the three letters I have provided a brief introduction that explains the historical circumstances and literary structure of the letter: the "who, when, where, what, and why" issues. Then, for each passage I present the text according to the New American Bible (revised edition, 1988) and an exposition of the text. The exposition works on three levels. For each passage it deals with literary matters: context, literary form, structure, words and images, and content. It also provides historical information where necessary about the circumstances, sources, parallel texts, cultural assumptions, and so forth. Furthermore, it seeks to clarify and highlight Paul's theological ideas, since Paul was a pastoral theologian who tried to help his people with advice rooted in and based on the gospel.

For Christians, the task of biblical interpretation cannot remain an exercise in historical research. For us these texts are part of the canon (authoritative collection) of Holy Scripture. We meditate on these texts and pray over them. And so for each letter I have included a section on its significance for Christian life.

This latter section consists of three parts. The first part ("Imaginative Recreation") is an exercise in using the imagination by identifying with the original recipients of these three letters. Having understood the literary, historical, and theological dimensions of the text, we now stand back and try to imagine how we as members of the community that first received the Pauline letter would have heard it and responded to it. The exercise here is a variation of Ignatian contemplation—the approach suggested by Ignatius Loyola in his *Spiritual Exercises* who urged the exercitants to imagine themselves as observers at a Gospel scene and to consider what they might see, hear, smell, touch, think, and feel.

The second part ("Points for Meditation") calls attention to the most important theological contributions of the letter, usually in the areas of Christology (who Christ is), ecclesiology (the Church), and ethics (Christian life). These central themes can be topics for meditation in which we try to discern what the biblical text may be saying to us as individuals, as a community of faith, or as a Church.

The third part ("Prayer") expresses briefly what we may want to say to God on the basis of this biblical text. The prayer typically gives thanks to God for what the text reveals about Christ Jesus, the Church, and Christian life. Then it asks for divine help in facing up to the challenges that the text may pose to our attitudes and behavior.

The procedure adopted in reading these texts combines the methods of biblical exegesis (literary, historical, and theological analysis) and the actualization of Scripture through *lectio divina* (reverent reading and imaginative appropriation, meditation, prayer, and action).

The process suggested for reading these three short letters can and should be applied to the individual parts. The language in these Pauline texts is rich, and each passage deserves appropriation, meditation, and prayer. Having seen the method at work once on a large scale (three short letters of one, four, and four chapters), one can then apply it to the individual units that make up the letters.

The method involves asking and answering four questions: What does this text say? What is God saying to me through this text? What do I want to say to God in response? What might God be asking me to do through this text? The expositions that constitute the bulk of this book will help especially in answering the first question. How one answers the other questions is part of the challenge of making Scripture the living word of God in Christian life.

The goal of the three chapters that follow is not only to provide information about three of Paul's prison letters but also to illustrate how to read these texts in an intelligent and prayerful manner.

I

The Letter to Philemon

Because it is addressed (primarily) to an individual and is the shortest text, Paul's letter to Philemon comes last in the traditional presentation of thirteen Pauline letters (which are arranged by length—first to communities and then to individuals). There is no real doubt that Paul composed this letter. Paul wrote to Philemon and his companions from prison. He refers to himself as a prisoner (1, 9), a captive (23), and in chains for the gospel (10, 13). For the problem about where Paul was imprisoned (Ephesus, Caesarea, Rome, etc.), see the discussion in the Introduction. The place of Paul's imprisonment obviously influences the precise dating of the letter. Ephesus around A.D. 55 is most likely. At any rate, the date must be in the 50s or the very early 60s of the first century A.D. And so the letter is an early witness to the theological language and church structures of the Pauline communities.

The common reading of the letter assumes that the main addressee was Philemon, who owned a slave named Onesimus. Philemon had been brought to Christian faith by Paul (19), perhaps at Ephesus. It appears that Philemon now lived at Colossae and allowed his fellow Christians to gather at his house. When Paul was in prison, Onesimus, the runaway slave of Philemon, approached Paul and became a Christian (10). If we are to imagine a real incarceration for Paul, then Onesimus might have met Paul as a fellow prisoner. If we are to imagine a freer kind of house arrest (which seems more likely), then Onesimus may have sought Paul out either because he already knew him through Philemon or had heard about him.

After Onesimus proved himself to be a sincere Christian (11), Paul agreed to write to Philemon on Onesimus' behalf as he sent him back to Philemon's household. The thrust of Paul's appeal was that Philemon should show his Christian love by taking back the slave Onesimus as a beloved "brother" (16). Paul even proposes to make restitution for what financial loss Onesimus brought to Philemon through his absence or through thievery (17-20). Paul's final appeal to Philemon to "do even more than I say" (21) may imply that Philemon was expected to set Onesimus free and/or send him back to Paul in prison. Paul the prisoner apparently had the freedom to carry on his ministry and to keep up his correspondence. He expected to be released soon and planned to visit Philemon (22). He had contact with several co-workers in Christ (23-24) and seemed to be in no danger of death.

Paul's letter to Philemon follows the basic outline found in other New Testament letters: greeting from the sender to the recipients (1-3), thanksgiving and petition (4-7), the body of the letter (8-20), and the closing (21-25). The letter purports to be from both Paul and Timothy (1). But it soon moves into first-person discourse in which the speaker is clearly Paul. It is addressed to Philemon, Apphia, and Archippus, as well as "the church at your house" (1-2). But it soon addresses one person, presumably Philemon. Though it is basically a communication between Paul and Philemon, it is nonetheless not a private letter. It is expected that the content will be known by the other addressees and perhaps was already known by Paul's co-workers listed in 23-24.

Paul's letter to Philemon is an excellent example of the New Testament letter form and a good introduction to Paul himself. On the one hand, Paul follows the conventions of the letter form and of deliberative rhetoric. On the other hand, Paul's language is emotional and personal—from the "heart" (see 7, 12, 20). Although he leaves Philemon free to make his own decision, he puts pressure on him by calling on his fellow addressees (even "the church at your house") and his co-workers (23-24). He praises Philemon publicly as a model of Christian faith expressing itself in love. And then he asks Philemon to prove himself once again by accepting his slave Onesimus as his beloved brother.

Greeting (1-3)

> [1]Paul, a prisoner for Christ Jesus, and Timothy our brother, to Philemon, our beloved brother and our co-worker, [2]to Apphia our sister, to Archippus our fellow soldier, and to the church at your house. [3]Grace to you and peace from God our Father and the Lord Jesus Christ.

Paul's greeting follows the customary pattern adopted in the Pauline letters: the name(s) of the sender(s), the identification of the recipients, and the greeting "grace and peace." This pattern was current among people of the Greco-Roman world (including Jews), and was adapted by Christians to bring out certain distinctive Christian beliefs.

Instead of Paul's usual designation of himself as an "apostle," here he calls himself a "prisoner for Christ Jesus" (see also 9, 10, 13), and so alludes to the sacrifice that he is making on behalf of the gospel and prepares for his appeal to Philemon on Onesimus' behalf in the body of the letter. Although Timothy appears in the greeting as Paul's co-author (as in 2 Corinthians, Philippians, Colossians, and 1 and 2 Thessalonians [with Silvanus]), as the letter proceeds Paul uses first-person language ("I") and drops any reference to Timothy.

The fact that the letter is addressed to three individuals (Philemon, Apphia, Archippus) and to "the church at your house" implies that Paul envisioned some kind of public reading. Philemon became a Christian through Paul's agency (19), acquired a good reputation among Christians (5, 7), and made his house available as a meeting place for the local Christian community (perhaps at Colossae, see Col 4:9, 17). Apphia was probably Philemon's wife. It is doubtful that Archippus was their son. The designation of Philemon as a "co-worker" and of Archippus as a "fellow soldier" indicates their active participation in the Christian mission (see Col 4:17).

The early Christians gathered for meetings and worship (including the eucharist) at the homes of members whose houses were large enough to accommodate them (see Rom 16:5; 1 Cor 16:9; Col 4:15). Estimates of how many people could gather at even a large house of the time vary between twenty and fifty. The "church" at someone's house was open not only to members of the household but also to outsiders, including slaves. See 1 Corinthians 11:17-34 for the social problems that arose in such settings.

The greeting "grace and peace" appears in all the Pauline letters. It combines the usual Jewish greeting "peace" (*shalom*) and the usual Greek greeting "grace" (*charis*). Paul tends to expand the customary greeting in terms of Christian beliefs ("from God our Father and the Lord Jesus Christ"). The divine favor and peace that were expected by Jews to mark the fullness of God's kingdom are now available through Jesus' death and resurrection.

The formulaic character of the greeting in Philemon 1-3 should not obscure Paul's rhetorical strategy. Despite the traditional title (Paul's letter to Philemon) this is not a private letter. In the first place, its body is somewhat longer than those of private letters in antiquity were. Moreover, it is addressed not only to Philemon but also to Apphia, Archippus, and the church at Philemon's house. Paul reminds them all that he is a "prisoner for Christ Jesus" and stresses the bonds that exist between them ("our co-worker," "our sister," "our fellow solider"). His goal is that they all accept the runaway slave Onesimus as a beloved brother (16). Thus what may seem to be a private letter is in fact quite public in its addressees and in the setting in which it will be received (the assembly of local Christians). The greeting puts pressure on Philemon to "do the right thing."

Thanksgiving and Petition (4-7)

4 I give thanks to my God always, remembering you in my prayers, 5 as I hear of the love and the faith you have in the Lord Jesus and for all the holy ones, 6 so that your partnership in the faith may become effective in recognizing every good there is in us that leads to Christ. 7 For I have experienced much joy and encouragement

20

from your love, because the hearts of the holy ones have been refreshed by you, brother.

The themes of thanksgiving and prayer intertwine in 4-7. Paul first expresses his thanks to God for Philemon (4a) and mentions his remembrance of him in prayer (4b). Next he explains why he is so thankful—because of Philemon's love and faith (5). Then he prays that Philemon's faith and knowledge may show themselves in love (6). Finally he returns to the theme of thanksgiving— because of Philemon's love and the impact that it has on Paul and on other Christians ("the saints," that is, those who have been made holy through contact with the Holy One).

In Greco-Roman letters of Paul's time, the address and greeting were often followed by a thanksgiving to the gods for the good health of the recipient and/or of the sender. This convention entered Hellenistic Judaism (as 2 Maccabees 1:10-11 shows). The thanksgiving is part of all the Pauline letters except Galatians where its absence and its replacement in Galatians 1:6 by an indication of astonishment ("I am amazed") are part of Paul's rhetorical strategy. The reasons for Paul's thanksgivings are never quite the same, though they usually concern growth in faith and love within the community. And a petition or a hope is usually included in the thanksgiving.

The Pauline thanksgivings are not purely formulaic. Paul the pastor adapted his thanksgivings to the achievements and failures of the communities that he addressed. Moreover, he often used the thanksgiving to express the key words and themes that are developed in the body of the letter—like an overture to a symphony.

The thanksgiving in Paul's letter to Philemon is more personal than those in other letters. Paul speaks in the first person ("I," "my God," etc.) and appears to lose sight of the addressees other than Philemon ("the love and the faith you have"). The key word in this thanksgiving is "love" (5, 7). Paul has heard about Philemon's love (maybe from Onesimus or Epaphras; see Col 1:7-8; 4:12). And he recalls how he and other Christians have been refreshed by it. In the main part of the letter Paul will appeal to Philemon's Christian love to accept Onesimus as his beloved brother in Christ (16). The vivid term "heart" (actually "innards" or "guts") in 7 appears in 12 with reference to Onesimus and in 20 in Paul's final appeal to Philemon.

The theology underlying this thanksgiving is the relation between faith/understanding and loving action. Paul portrays Philemon as a model Christian distinguished for his faith toward Jesus and his love toward other Christians (5). His prayer (6) is that in the case of Onesimus Philemon's faith and knowledge of what God has done in Christ (and continues to do) will once more prove themselves in loving action. Paul appeals not to his authority as an apostle or to his status as Philemon's "spiritual father" but rather to the faith and love that they share in Christ.

The Body of the Letter (vv. 8-20)

[8]Therefore, although I have the full right in Christ to order you to do what is proper, [9]I rather urge you out of love, being as I am, Paul, an old man, and now also a prisoner for Christ Jesus. [10]I urge you on behalf of my child Onesimus, whose father I have become in my imprisonment, [11]who was once useless to you but is now

useful to [both] you and me. [12] I am sending him, that is, my own heart, back to you.

[13] I should have liked to retain him for myself, so that he might serve me on your behalf in my imprisonment for the gospel, [14] but I did not want to do anything without your consent, so that the good you do might not be forced but voluntary. [15] Perhaps this is why he was away from you for a while, that you might have him back forever, [16] no longer as a slave but more than a slave, a brother, beloved especially to me, but even more so to you, as a man and in the Lord.

[17] So if you regard me as a partner, welcome him as you would me. [18] And if he has done you any injustice or owes you anything, charge it to me. [19] I, Paul, write this in my own hand; I will pay. May I not tell you that you owe me your very self. [20] Yes, brother, may I profit from you in the Lord. Refresh my heart in Christ.

The body of the letter is in three parts. First in 8-12 Paul explains his approach to Philemon as an appeal rather than an order (8-10) and recounts his own involvement with Onesimus (11-12). Paul the prisoner brought Onesimus to Christian faith and is now sending him back to Philemon in the hope that he will be received as a beloved brother and will live up to the meaning of his name (in Greek "Onesimus" means "useful"). Then in 13-16 Paul explains why he is sending Onesimus back to Philemon (13-14) and speculates on God's purposes in this affair, especially with regard to Onesimus' new status as a beloved brother to Paul and Philemon (15-16). Finally in 17-20 Paul uses business and legal images to express his request: "Welcome him as you would me" (17). As a partner in Christian faith, Paul promises to make good whatever is owed to Philemon on account of Onesimus' absence. At the same time Paul reminds Philemon how much he owes to Paul.

Slavery was an accepted social institution in the Roman empire. A slave who ran away from a master's household had several options: turn to banditry, disappear into the subculture of a large city, flee far away, seek other menial (chiefly agricultural) work, or seek asylum at a shrine or temple. It was customary to pursue runaway slaves and to reward those who captured them or aided in their capture.

By law Paul had an obligation to send back the runaway slave Onesimus to his master Philemon, though he could presumably have asked to retain Onesimus and his services on the basis of his past relationship with Philemon and his present imprisonment for the gospel. In closing the letter Paul expresses confidence that Philemon "will do even more than I say" (21). This is often taken to mean that Philemon was expected to free Onesimus from slavery and/or send him back to Paul to serve as his assistant. But this is far from certain (see 1 Cor 7:20-24, "Everyone should remain in the state in which he was called").

In making his request, Paul is careful to preserve Philemon's independence, while nonetheless pushing him to act in a certain way. On the one hand, he makes a request and does not give an order (8-10). He complies with Roman law by sending back a runaway slave (12). He wants Philemon to decide of his own free will (14). On the other hand, his request is based on Christian love (9) and on God's will (15-16). And he does appeal for sympathy on the basis of his own condition ("an old man, and now also a prisoner for Christ Jesus," 9) and uses a highly emotional term for "heart" (7, 12, 20) in referring to the case. The business and legal images in 17-20 echo what was said about sharing faith in love in 6. The "bottom line" of the business metaphor is that Philemon owes so much to Paul that he should comply with his request to receive Onesimus back and to look upon him as his beloved brother.

Closing (21-25)

> [21] With trust in your compliance I write to you, knowing that you will do even more than I say. [22] At the same time prepare a guest room for me, for I hope to be granted to you through your prayers. [23] Epaphras, my fellow prisoner in Christ Jesus, greets you, [24] as well as Mark, Aristarchus, Demas, and Luke, my co-workers. [25] The grace of the Lord Jesus Christ be with your spirit.

After expressing confidence that Philemon will comply with Paul's request (21), the closing of the letter alludes to Paul's plan to visit Philemon after his release from captivity (22). Then it conveys greetings from other Christians who are with Paul (23-24) and offers a concluding prayer (25). This closing conveys in a short space features that appear near the end of almost all of Paul's letters: travel plans, personal greetings, and a concluding prayer. These features give us an insight into the network of communication that existed in the Pauline churches, and in the case of this letter are integral to Paul's rhetorical strategy to convince Philemon to do the right thing.

By expressing his expectation that Philemon will comply with his request (21), Paul is not suddenly pulling rank and demanding obedience to his apostolic authority. Rather, obedience is owed to Christian faith expressed in loving deeds, not to Paul (see 6). However, by announcing his plans to visit Philemon's house in the near future (22), he certainly adds to the pressure on Philemon. When he arrives, Paul will be able to see for himself what has happened with Onesimus.

We can presume that those to whom the letter was addressed knew Paul's fellow prisoner Epaphras and the other co-workers (23-24). All these names appear also in the personal greetings in Colossians 4:10-14, where further information is supplied about them. The list reminds Philemon that the case of Onesimus is well known among the members of Paul's ministerial team. These persons in turn presumably have friends in the community that meets at Philemon's household. The use of the plural form in the final blessing in 25 ("with your spirit") reaffirms the public character of the letter (see 1-3), and reminds Philemon that all the Christians there are watching to see what he will do.

Philemon in Christian Life

Imaginative Recreation: Thus far we have worked through the text of Paul's letter to Philemon with particular attention to its literary features and its historical setting. Before proceeding to the letter's theological and pastoral themes, it may be useful to engage in an exercise of the imagination.

Imagine that you are a member of the "house church" that met at Philemon's home. You have heard that a letter from the apostle Paul has just arrived and will be read this evening at the gathering of Christians. You have heard that it concerns that "useless" slave Onesimus who ran away from Philemon's household. About forty Christians—men and women, Jews and Gentiles, slaves and free—are in the room. The letter is produced, and a designated man begins to read it.

The letter is short but full of surprises. It is addressed not only to Philemon but to all of us. That is why it is now being read publicly. It seems that Onesimus has become a Christian under Paul's instruction. It seems that Paul wants Philemon to take Onesimus back "no longer as a slave but more than a slave, a brother!" Imagine that you are a slave and hear those words. Imagine that you are a slaveowner and hear those words. Imagine how Philemon feels now as he is being put on the spot publicly to do as Paul requests.

Points for Meditation: Even though Paul's letter to Philemon has been criticized for lacking serious theological content, in fact there is much practical theology to be gained from it. The basic theological principle underlying the letter is that Christian faith must express itself in deeds of love. The key word is "love." Philemon who is distinguished already for his deeds of love (5, 7) is urged to take Onesimus back as his "beloved" brother (16). What has happened through Jesus' death and resurrection (justification, salvation, redemption, and so forth) needs to be appropriated through faith, which in turn shows itself in deeds of love. What Paul asks Philemon to do is a concrete example of faith expressing itself in love.

Paul asks Philemon to accept Onesimus as his beloved brother (16). The debate about whether Paul expected him to free Onesimus should not distract us from the certain and central concern of the letter: Philemon is being asked to look upon his slave Onesimus as his equal in the eyes of God, as one who shared equally with Paul and Philemon the "new creation" brought about by Christ in which there is "neither slave nor free" (see Gal 3:28). It is easy for us to read all this with a sense of moral superiority. After all, we no longer allow slavery. But in the U.S.A. that moral enlightenment came only 130 years ago! The real lesson of Paul's letter to Philemon is the equality and kinship we share in Christ before God. There are differences in gender, in social and economic status, and in ethnic background. But more important than all these obvious differences are the fundamental equality and kinship we have before God in Christ. We all are one in Christ: Jew and Greek, slave and free, male and female. And therefore we should be prepared to recognize that what is truly important about our fellow Christians is not their race or ethnic history, not their social or economic status, and not their gender, but rather our fundamental dignity as God's people in Christ.

Paul's letter to Philemon also gives us insight into early Church life: the house church as the locus of activity, the close emotional ties between apostle and converts, the varied social classes represented in a local church, the network of communication among the communities, and the common faith as the ultimate authority. Though small in size, Paul's letter to Philemon yields important information about being an early Christian.

Prayer: God the Father of our Lord Jesus Christ, I thank you for the gift of Christian faith, for membership in the world-wide body of Christ, and for what I share with peoples of every race and nation, of every social and economic class. Help me to express my faith in deeds of love, give me understanding and openness of heart toward all my Christian brothers and sisters, and increase my courage to work against all kinds of prejudice and discrimination in our Church and in our world. Amen.

II

The Letter to the Philippians

Philippi in northeastern Greece took its name from King Philip II of Macedon (359-336 B.C.), the father of Alexander the Great. After the Roman conquest of Macedonia in 168-167 B.C., Philippi became a major stop on the Via Egnatia, the major highway that connected Asia Minor (present-day Turkey) with Italy. In the first century B.C. it was refounded as a Roman colony and governed by Italian law. The religious life of the city apparently included the cults of both Roman and Greek deities.

According to Acts 16:12-40, Paul came to Philippi and there founded his first European Christian community. In Acts 16:12 the place is described as "a leading city in that district of Macedonia and a Roman colony." The initial success of Paul's mission here was due in large part to Lydia and other women who gathered with her. Lydia is described as a "worshiper of God" (Acts 16:14). In Acts that most likely means that she was a Gentile who was very interested in Judaism but had not yet fully converted to it. The stories about Paul and Silas in Philippi bring out the Roman character of the law code and administration of the city (see Acts 16:20-21, 35-38). The apostle's search for a place of prayer on the Sabbath and their finding only a group of women outside the city along the river (16:13) suggest at best a very small Jewish presence.

After Paul had founded the Christian community at Philippi and moved on to other places, he remained in touch with the Philippian Christians by means of messengers and letters. He had great affection for these people—to the point that some scholars describe them as Paul's favorite community.

The letter to the Philippians bears the names of Paul and Timothy (1:1). By 1:3, however, Paul moves into first-person speech ("I") and later talks about Timothy in the third person ("he") in 2:19-24. When the letter was written in large part depends on the place of Paul's imprisonment. Since the text contains so many references to visits and travel plans, and since it supposes much communication between Paul and people at Philippi, it is unlikely that Paul was writing from such far away places as Rome or Caesarea Maritima in Palestine. The references to the "praetorium" in 1:13 and to "Caesar's household" in 4:22 are not decisive arguments in favor of Rome, since these institutions could be found in many provinical capitals of the Roman empire. Many scholars assume that Paul must have been imprisoned in Ephesus around A.D. 55. That city was a major center of the Pauline mission, and it is near enough to Philippi to explain the many contacts between Paul and the Philippians.

The letter to the Philippians follows the usual outline: greeting (1:1-2), thanksgiving and prayer (1:3-11), and so forth. But the body of the letter as we have it makes sharp transitions in content and tone—so much so that many interpreters regard it not as a single letter but rather as a collection of three letters.

In this theory the first letter in time is Paul's "thank you" note in 4:10-20. The second letter is the "main letter" contained in 1:1–3:1a and parts of chapter 4 (4:2-9, 21-23). Here Paul is in prison and reflects on the role of his imprisonment in spreading the gospel (1:12-26). He also gives instructions for promoting unity of hearts and minds within the Philippian community (1:27–2:18). In 2:6-11 he quotes an early Christian hymn about Christ in order to ground his advice in the example of Christ Jesus. Also included are the travel plans of his co-workers Timothy and Epaphroditus (2:19–3:1a), further instructions for the community (4:2-9), and farewells (4:21-23).

The third letter (3:1b–4:1) is more polemical in tone: "Beware of the dogs! Beware of the evil-workers! Beware of the mutilation!" (3:2). Here Paul is warning the Gentile Christians at Philippi against Jewish Christian missionaries who had an approach different from Paul's about the conditions for admitting non-Jews into the Church. They apparently expected Gentile Christians to become Jews by accepting circumcision and observing the Jewish food laws and Sabbath regulations. Paul contended that there was no need for Gentile Christians to become Jews, since their membership in the people of God came through their baptism into Jesus' death and resurrection. Paul faced the same kind of opposition in his letter to the Galatians and in 2 Corinthians. Nothing in this letter indicates that Paul is in prison. In fact, he may have been already released.

That Philippians may be a collection of three letters makes little difference to most readers, since in prayer and liturgy we usually take the text in small pieces. And not all scholars accept the three-letter hypothesis. But it does help to explain the rough transitions in the structure of the present text and can help us to track Paul's relations with his "favorite community." The exposition that follows proceeds according to the traditional order of the letter as it has come down to us. The imaginative exercise after the exposition will follow the "chronological order" of the three letters.

Greeting (1:1-2)

> [1] Paul and Timothy, slaves of Christ Jesus, to all the holy ones in Christ Jesus who are in Philippi, with the overseers and ministers: [2] grace to you and peace from God our Father and the Lord Jesus Christ.

The salutation in Philippians 1:1-2 follows the usual outline: the senders (Paul and Timothy), the addressees (all the "holy ones" in Philippi), and the greeting ("grace and peace"). Timothy also appears in the salutations of 2 Corinthians, 1 Thessalonians, and Philemon, as well as Colossians and 2 Thessalonians (whose authorship are disputed). Mention of him here prepares for what will be said about him in Philippians 2:19-24. Likewise, the description of Paul and Timothy as "slaves" may point forward to the description of Christ as a "slave" in Philippians 2:7. The name of Jesus appears three times in these two verses, twice prefaced by the term "Christ." The recipients are called the "saints" or "holy ones," a common early Christian designation for those made holy by God the Holy One through Christ. The conventional "grace and peace" formula is expanded by the distinctively Christian theological expression "God our Father and the Lord Jesus Christ."

The most distinctive and intriguing feature of the greeting in Philippians 1:1-2, however, is the reference to "overseers and ministers." There is no evidence that the phrase is a later textual addition. In Greek these two terms are *episkopoi* (usually translated as "bishops") and *diakonoi* (usually translated as "deacons"). Since this is the only reference to *episkopoi* in Paul's seven undisputed letters and since Philippians is a very early document within the New Testament, this text has been of great interest.

What roles these officials played within the Christian community at Philippi is not certain. The word *episkopos* means "overseer." In Greco-Roman associations the term *episkopos* is connected with financial oversight, while the Hebrew equivalent in the Dead Sea scrolls (*mebaqqer*) implies a degree of spiritual leadership. The word *diakonos* means "servant" or "minister." It can refer to one who waits on tables (see Acts 6:1-6), to a minister of the gospel (2 Cor 6:4; 11:23), or to a Church official (1 Tm 3:8, 12). A Church order featuring the offices of *episkopos* and *diakonos* is taken for granted in 1 Timothy 3:1-13, though how the presbyters/elders relate to them remains unclear.

What is certain is that in the 50s of the first century A.D. the church at Philippi had *episkopoi* and *diakonoi*. Since there are more than one *episkopos* at Philippi, we are at a stage prior to the emergence of the monepiscopate or monarchical episcopate (= one bishop in a place). The plurality of "overseers" can be explained as due to the existence of several house churches or small groups at Philippi, or the need for several "overseers" for the community as a whole. Thus the reference to "overseers and ministers" in Philippians 1:1 provides evidence for the early existence of *episkopoi* and *diakonoi* in the Pauline communities, while reminding us that these offices were not necessarily yet what they later became in Church history.

Thanksgiving and Prayer (1:3-11)

[3] I give thanks to my God at every remembrance of you, [4] praying always with joy in my every prayer for all of you, [5] because of your partnership for the gospel from the first day until now. [6] I am confident of this, that the one who began a good work in you will continue to complete it until the day of Christ Jesus.

[7] It is right that I should think this way about all of you, because I hold you in my heart, you who are all partners with me in grace, both in my imprisonment and in the defense and confirmation of the gospel. [8] For God is my witness, how I long for all of you with the affection of Christ Jesus.

[9] And this is my prayer that your love may increase ever more and more in knowledge and every kind of perception, [10] to discern what is of value, so that you may be pure and blameless for the day of Christ, [11] filled with the fruit of righteousness that comes through Jesus Christ for the glory and praise of God.

For the formulas and conventions of the Pauline thanksgiving, see the discussion of Philemon 4-7. Here as elsewhere Paul joins expressions of thanksgiving to God for the Christians at Philippi with prayers on their behalf.

First in Philippians 1:3-6 Paul (now using first-person language) gives thanks to God because the Philippians have shared in his gospel ministry right from the start. Whether this refers to the beginning of Paul's activity in Macedonia, or to the Philippians' first contacts with Paul, is not clear. Paul also mentions his continuous prayer on their behalf (1:3b-4) and expresses confidence in God's care for them right up to "the day of Christ Jesus" (1:6). The fourfold use of "every ... always ... every ... all" in 1:3-4 heightens the emotional tone. The word "joy" in 1:4

expresses a major theme of the letter as a whole. The word "gospel" in 1:5 refers not only to the message focused on Jesus' death and resurrection (see Rom 1:3-4; 1 Cor 15:3-5) but also to the missionary activity undertaken in spreading that message.

Then in 1:7-8 Paul expresses his great affection for the Philippian Christians in highly emotional terms and alludes to his own situation as a prisoner for the gospel. The term "think" in 1:7 anticipates another major theme of the letter. Though a verb of thinking and knowing, it also has an emotional side ("feel"). What Paul thinks/feels is all that has been mentioned in 1:3-6. After a concrete reference to his imprisonment in 1:7 Paul refers to his public defense of the gospel, perhaps in some kind of formal legal proceeding ("the defense and confirmation of the gospel"). The reference to the Philippians as "partners" and the threefold use of "all" in 1:7-8 continue the emotional tone set in 1:3-6. This is further strengthened by the emotional verb "long for" and the very forceful noun "innards, guts" (*splanchna*) in 1:8, rendered as "affection" here and as "heart" in Philemon 7, 12, 20.

Finally in 1:9-11 Paul prays that the Philippian Christians may grow in love and spiritual insight so that in the present they may do good and at the "day of Christ" they may be found faultless. What is said in 1:9-11 gives the content of Paul's habitual prayer on the Philippians' behalf that was mentioned in 1:3-4. See Philemon 6 and Colossians 1:9-14 for similar prayers at this point in a Pauline letter. In 1:9 the terms "knowledge" (see Phlm 6; Col 1:9-10; 2:2; 3:10; Eph 1:17; 4:13) and "perception" cover the full range of intellectual and moral reasoning. The power to discern what really matters in 1:10 is the result of the knowledge and perception referred to in 1:9. The goal is to appear morally pure and faultless on judgment day. The expression "fruit of righteousness" in 1:11 most likely has the same sense as the "fruit of the Spirit" in Galatians 5:22-23. The idea is that good actions proceed from the righteousness that comes through Christ. The goal of such actions is the glory and praise of God.

One of the important functions of the thanksgivings in the Pauline letters is to introduce some of the major themes developed in the body of the letter. One such theme is the apostle's joy even in the midst of suffering: "praying always with joy" (1:4). For other uses of the noun "joy" in the letter, see 1:25; 2:2, 29; 4:1. For the verb "rejoice" see 1:18; 2:17-18, 28; 3:1; 4:4. Despite (or because of) his sufferings as a prisoner for the gospel, Paul finds reasons for joy.

Paul gives thanks to God because the Philippians have shared in the "gospel" (1:5) and so are his "partners" in grace (1:7). Paul views himself as engaged in the defense and confirmation of the gospel (1:7). This emphasis on the "gospel" prepares for Paul's own estimate of the results of his imprisonment in 1:12-26: It has advanced the gospel. It also prepares for his plans for carrying on the apostolic mission through the labors of Timothy and Epaphroditus in 2:19-30.

The occurrence of the verb "think" in 1:7 is the first occurrence of the term *phroneō* that runs through the letter. Though difficult to translate the same way in each instance, the verb is prominent in Paul's exhortation to unity within the community in 1:27–2:18. The unity of minds and hearts that Paul so earnestly seeks among the Philippians will come from "thinking one thing" (2:2), which in turn is based on having "the same attitude" in Christ Jesus as he is presented in the early Christian hymn preserved in 2:6-11.

Paul's references to the day of Christ Jesus (1:6, 10) are in the context of the letter as a whole not merely formulaic correctives to an overemphasis on the present. Paul the prisoner sees death as a real possibility for himself (see 1:20-23) and reflects on what it means to "depart this life and be with Christ" (1:23). In his exhortation to the Philippians (2:16) Paul also expresses the hope that he will be able to point to their spiritual accomplishments as an indication that his own apostolic ministry was fruitful.

Another important function of the Pauline thanksgivings is to introduce the main characters and their relationships. This task is carried out most clearly in 1:7-8. There Paul explains that he is imprisoned and hints that he is involved in a trial or some other legal proceeding at which he must defend and confirm the gospel. Besides describing his own situation, Paul also expresses the deep affection that he has for the Philippian Christians: "I hold you in my heart ... how I long for all of you." The basis of his affection is their common experience of Christ Jesus, which has made them "partners ... in grace." This intimate relationship will serve as the foundation for Paul's remarks about his own situation and his advice to the Philippians in the body of the letter. Paul's warm feelings toward the Philippian Christians come out also in his comments about continuing prayer on their behalf (1:3-4) and in the text of the prayer in 1:9-11. What he wishes for them is the fullness of Christian life: love, knowledge, discernment, good deeds flowing from righteousness, and vindication at the last judgment.

Paul's Past and Present (1:12-18a)

¹² I want you to know, brothers, that my situation has turned out rather to advance the gospel, ¹³ so that my imprisonment has become well known in Christ throughout the whole praetorium and to all the rest, ¹⁴ and so that the majority of the brothers, having taken encouragement in the Lord from my imprisonment, dare more than ever to proclaim the word fearlessly.

¹⁵ Of course, some preach Christ from envy and rivalry, others from good will. ¹⁶ The latter act out of love, aware that I am here for the defense of the gospel; ¹⁷ the former proclaim Christ out of selfish ambition, not from pure motives, thinking that they will cause me trouble in my imprisonment. ¹⁸ What difference does it make, as long as in every way, whether in pretense or in truth, Christ is being proclaimed?

In the next two sections Paul discusses what has already happened to him and his present situation (1:12-18a), and reflects on his future (1:18b-26). He gives few concrete details, mainly because he is more interested in interpreting what has taken place and what will take place. His fundamental concern is how these events affect the spreading of the gospel.

He first expresses his conviction that his imprisonment has contributed to the advance of the gospel (1:12). His use of the formula "I want you to know" early in his letter (see Gal 1:11; 2 Cor 1:8; Rom 1:13) gives emphasis to this conviction. The most obvious referent of "my situation" is Paul's imprisonment and the legal proceedings in which he is involved (see 1:7). He interprets his imprisonment as the occasion for the advance of the gospel (its content and the mission of communicating it to others) not only outside the Church (1:13) but also inside the Church (1:14-17).

First he shows how his imprisonment has influenced those outside the Church (1:13). His imprisonment for his Christian faith ("in Christ") became known throughout the whole "praetorium"—originally a term for a Roman general's tent and later used to describe the residence of an imperial governor such as Pontius Pilate (see Mt 27:27; Mk 15:16; Jn 18:28, 33; 19:9) and Felix (Acts 23:25). As these examples indicate, the term does not demand a setting in Rome or in the imperial household there.

Then Paul shows in greater detail how his imprisonment has contributed to the progress of the Christian mission. He first refers to those Christians who seem positively disposed toward him (the "majority") and have been led by Paul's example to preach the gospel even more fearlessly (1:14). Then in 1:15-17 he describes those who preach Christ out of "envy and rivalry."

The lack of details about Paul's imprisonment and defense of the gospel can be explained in various ways. Perhaps those bringing the letter to the Philippians could explain the details. Perhaps Paul did not want to give out too much information, lest he anger the Roman officials. Perhaps Paul did not regard these details as important. What emerges from this passage is someone more interested in the "advance" of the gospel than in his own well being. He finds in his imprisonment the providential hand of God. Because his imprisonment has spread the gospel to those in the praetorium and to others, and incited his Christian friends and critics to greater activity on behalf of the gospel, Paul can rejoice even in his chains (1:18a).

The identity of the critics is not specified. They are surely Christians, since they proclaim Christ (1:17). Paul impugns their motives by attributing their actions to "envy and rivalry" (1:15) and "selfish ambition" or perhaps "contentiousness" (1:17). According to Paul they want to add to his suffering in prison (1:17). The most likely candidates are the Jewish Christians under attack in Philippians 3:2. These people may have seen God's hand at work in Paul's imprisonment, so as to silence Paul and his Law-free gospel for the Gentiles. Paul turns the tables on them by arguing that his imprisonment has inspired his critics to greater zeal, with the result that the gospel is now being preached even more vigorously. And that is all that Paul wanted!

The conviction that the gospel is being preached in all these ways leads Paul to a tolerance toward those who oppose and criticize him (see Mk 9:38-40; Lk 9:49-50). In 3:2, however, Paul attacks his opponents and even ridicules them. It is possible that in the course of composing his letter, Paul grew more daring in his criticism of his Jewish Christian rivals. Or perhaps there was a space of time between the writing of the two texts, and some further provocations had occurred (see the discussion of Philippians 3 below).

Paul's Future (1:18b-26)

> Indeed I shall continue to rejoice, [19] for I know that this will result in deliverance for me through your prayers and support from the Spirit of Jesus Christ. [20] My eager expectation and hope is that I shall not be put to shame in any way, but that with all boldness, now as always, Christ will be magnified in my body, whether by life or by death.

²¹For to me life is Christ, and death is gain. ²²If I go on living in the flesh, that means fruitful labor for me. And I do not know which I shall choose. ²³I am caught between the two. I long to depart this life and be with Christ, [for] that is far better. ²⁴Yet that I remain [in] the flesh is more necessary for your benefit.

²⁵This I know with confidence, that I shall remain and continue in the service of all of you for your progress and joy in the faith, ²⁶so that your boasting in Christ Jesus may abound on account of me when I come to you again.

After reflecting on past events and his present situation (1:12-18a), Paul considers the possible fates that await him in the future. His basic principle, "life is Christ" (1:21), allows him to consider both death and continued life on earth as good. The reflection moves from Paul's present imprisonment and upcoming trial (1:19-20), through a philosophical/theological meditation on Christian life and death (1:21-24), to a confident affirmation that he expects to be released and allowed to resume his activity as an apostle (1:25-26).

The reflection begins and ends on a note of "joy" (1:18b, 25). The nature of the "deliverance" (1:19; see Jb 13:16) that Paul expects is a matter of controversy. Is it the spiritual salvation that accompanies Christian death and the fullness of life with God (as is suggested by 1:21-24)? Or is it release from imprisonment after Paul's legal case has been heard and judged (as is suggested by 1:25-26)? As Paul faces his trial with "eager expectation" (see also Rom 8:19), his major concern is that Christ will "be magnified" (1:20)—whether through Paul's life or through his death. This concern carries on Paul's total dedication to the spreading of the gospel that was so prominent in the preceding section. Though Paul expects to be acquitted (see 1:25-26), he is not totally certain of the outcome (as "by death" in 1:20 indicates).

The philosophical/theological reflection on living and dying begins with the principle "to me life is Christ" (1:21a). For Paul and other Christians, eternal life begins with initiation into Christ at baptism. Then Paul gives two options: "death is gain" (1:21b) and living on "in the flesh" (used neutrally here, not negatively) allows for further apostolic activity (1:22a). Death is a gain because it can bring an even greater closeness to Christ. Then he observes how hard it is to choose between the two (1:22b-23a), though ultimately it is to be God's choice and not Paul's. Finally, Paul declares that dying and being with Christ is better from his personal perspective (1:23b), whereas continuing to serve as an apostle "in the flesh" is better from the perspective of the Philippian Christians (1:24). Being with Christ implies a form of Christ's presence different from and more powerful than that brought about in baptism. It suggests an afterlife existence like that described in 2 Corinthians 4:16–5:10. This new mode of existence appears to take place before the fullness of God's kingdom is revealed on the last day (compare 1 Cor 15 and 1 Thes 4:13–5:11).

The general context of Paul's reflection on living and dying in 1:21-24 may be Greek and Latin ideas about life and the flesh being burdens from which one is freed in death. There may even be some connection with philo-sophical debates on the possibility and desirablity of suicide (the "noble death"). But such parallels can blur what is distinctively Christian about Paul's reflection. For

Paul, eternal life had already begun. Death will bring an intensification of life in Christ, not an end or even a beginning of it. Paul's apparent "indifference" therefore is based on his conviction that eternal life with Christ has already started.

In 1:25-26 Paul returns to the concrete situation of his imprisonment and expresses the conviction that he will be freed so as to take up again his work as an apostle of Jesus Christ. This expectation is a further indication that Paul was probably not far away from Philippi (perhaps in Ephesus) rather than in Rome or in Caesarea Maritima. If he was imprisoned in Ephesus, then it is likely that he was released and that he again visited the Philippians as he promised (1:26). Just as Paul had declared his imprisonment to be for the advance of the gospel (1:12) and a source of joy (1:4, 18), so he expresses confidence that his further apostolic work will contribute to "your progress and joy in the faith" (1:25).

Unity in the Christian Community (1:27–2:4)

[27] Only, conduct yourselves in a way worthy of the gospel of Christ, so that, whether I come and see you or am absent, I may hear news of you, that you are standing firm in one spirit, with one mind struggling together for the faith of the gospel, [28] not intimidated in any way by your opponents. This is proof to them of destruction, but of your salvation. And this is God's doing. [29] For to you has been granted, for the sake of Christ, not only to believe in him but also to suffer for him. [30] Yours is the same struggle as you saw in me and now hear about me.

[2:1] If there is any encouragement in Christ, any solace in love, any participation in the Spirit, any compassion and mercy, [2]complete my joy by being of the same mind, with the same love, united in heart, thinking one thing. [3]Do nothing out of selfishness or out of vainglory; rather, humbly regard others as more important than yourselves, [4]each looking out not for his own interests, but [also] everyone for those of others.

At this point in the letter Paul moves from his own situation to that of the Philippians. He first urges them to spiritual unity (1:27–2:4), then sets before them the example of Christ the Servant (2:5-11), and finally gives further exhortations (2:12-18). The first part of the first section (1:27–2:4) deals with the threat from outside the community (1:27-30) and then with the ideal of unity within the community (2:1-4).

Having expressed his confidence that he will visit the Philippians again (1:26), Paul urges them to conduct themselves worthily of the gospel so that he will either see or hear about their steadfast unity in the gospel. The "faith of the gospel" (1:27) refers to the faith that is constituted by and summarized in the proclamation of the good news about Jesus' death and resurrection.

The identity of the "opponents" in 1:28 is not entirely clear. Though they could be non-Christians, most interpreters link them to Paul's Jewish Christian rivals and view them as basically the same people who are attacked in 1:15, 17 and 3:2, 18-19. If this is so, then the (Pauline) gospel opposed by them probably emphasized (excessively in their opinion) the cross of Christ (see also 1 Cor 1–4). Paul suggests that the opponents see in the cross only a sign of "destruction" whereas according to Paul the cross is really the sign of "salvation" (here surely to be taken in a spiritual sense). Paul's gospel stressed the cross of Christ, not the Jewish Law, as the way to right relationship with God for non-Jews (Gentiles). Paul is urging the largely Gentile Christian community at Philippi to remain faithful to the Law-free gospel that he had preached to them. This interpretation of the opponents would make more intelligible Paul's charge in 3:18 that the opponents are "enemies of the cross of Christ."

If the opponents are Jewish Christian missionaries and if their version of the gospel (that is, Gentile Christians must become Jews by undergoing circumcision and keeping the Jewish Law) was unsettling to the Gentile Christians of Philippi, Paul seeks to comfort the Philippians by associating their sufferings for the gospel with those of Christ (1:29) and with his own sufferings (1:30). For the idea of suffering "for the sake of Christ" (1:29), see also 2 Corinthians 12:10. Being a Christian involves not only believing in the gospel but also suffering and sharing in the cross as the God-given sign of deliverance. In 1:30 Paul's imprisonment and other sufferings are presented as examples of what the Philippians can expect. The term "struggle" may have an athletic nuance (see also "struggling together" in 1:27 and "run" in 2:16).

In 2:1-4 the perspective shifts to life within the community, though the threat of disunity apparently remains the same. From the perspective of grammar, 2:1-4 constitutes one long sentence: the basis for the exhortation ("if there is ..." 2:1), the main clause ("complete my joy," 2:2a), the exhortation to unity of hearts and minds within the community (2:2b), and humility and concern for others as the proper means toward such unity (2:3-4).

The assumption of the four "if" clauses in 2:1 is that all these conditions do exist in the Philippian community.

45

The terms are all quite emotional ("encouragement ... solace in love ... participation in the Spirit ... compassion and mercy"). These feelings are grounded in Christ and the Spirit. The main clause "complete my joy" in 2:2 develops the theme of "joy" already raised in connection with Paul's imprisonment in 1:4, 18, 25. The way by which Paul's joy will be made complete is through the Philippians' "being of the same mind" and "thinking one thing," echoing the theme raised in 1:7. The opposite of the attitude that Paul promotes is "vainglory" or "empty conceit" (2:3), which means having a false opinion about oneself. The attitude that Paul encourages involves putting aside one's own interests and looking out for the interests of others (2:4) after the example of Christ the Servant.

This text indicates the extent to which Paul regarded the gospel as something worth fighting for and how much he valued the union of hearts and minds within the Christian community. The language is emotional and highly charged. The key words are "joy" and "think." What is at stake are the Philippians' identity as Christians and their manner of dealing with one another within the community of faith.

The Case of Christ Jesus (2:5-11)

⁵ Have among yourselves the same attitude that is also yours in Christ Jesus,

⁶ Who, though he was in the form of God, did not regard equality with God something to be grasped. ⁷ Rather, he emptied himself, taking the form of a slave, coming in human likeness, and found human in appearance, ⁸ he humbled himself, becoming obedient to death, even death on a cross.

⁹Because of this, God greatly exalted him and bestowed on him the name that is above every name, ¹⁰that at the name of Jesus every knee should bend, of those in heaven and on earth and under the earth, ¹¹and every tongue confess that Jesus Christ is Lord, to the glory of God the Father.

By far the most famous part of Paul's letter to the Philippians is 2:5-11. It is widely held that Paul sought to resolve the disunity and tension within the Christian community at Philippi by quoting at this point an early Christian hymn about the humiliation and exaltation of Christ the Servant (2:6-11). That 2:6-11 represents the quotation of existing material is indicated by its somewhat awkward fit in its present context (with 2:5 as an introduction) and by its peculiar vocabulary ("form of God," "equality with God," "something to be grasped," etc.). That it was a hymn (or part of a hymn) is suggested by its use of parallelism and rhythmic speech. It is unlikely (though not entirely impossible) that Paul composed the hymn. It probably arose in the context of early Christian worship and thus tells us something concerning very early Christian beliefs about Jesus. The original language of the hymn may have been Aramaic (since the present Greek text can be translated back into Aramaic without much difficulty). Paul's letter to the Philippians comes from the mid-50s of the first century. Thus the theological language and concepts of 2:6-11 are especially important for understanding first-generation Christian beliefs about Jesus.

Many structural outlines have been proposed for 2:6-11. The most popular outline (which is followed here) distinguishes two stanzas of three verses each: the humiliation of Christ (2:6-8), and the exaltation of Christ (2:9-

11). The first stanza describes Christ's life as equal to or like God (2:6), his incarnation (2:7), and his death (2:8). Many interpreters regard "even death on a cross" in 2:8 as an additional comment by Paul or some other editor. The second stanza deals with the exaltation of Christ as Lord (2:9) and the homage paid to him by all creation (2:10-11). Another outline finds three stanzas of four lines each: Christ the perfect image of God (2:6-7b), Christ humbling himself and accepting death (2:7c-8), and the exaltation of Christ as Lord (2:9-11).

The hymn is introduced by a plea for having the "same attitude" as Christ had. The verb is the same term for "thinking" featured in 2:2 (see also 1:7). The idea is that the Philippians should make their own the attitude of humility and selflessness displayed by Christ in his incarnation and death on the cross.

The content of the hymn deserves careful attention. To say that Christ was "in the form of God" (2:6) refers to his outward appearance, shape, or condition that points to his essential status or character. In other words, Christ Jesus enjoyed a divine status. Though some interpreters find an allusion to Adam (see Gn 1:26-27), the expression is probably better taken as a description of Christ's divinity in terms of his pre-existence (see Col 1:15-20; Jn 1:1-18; Heb 1:3). Christ Jesus in his earthly life did not seek to be treated on a par with God. In other words, he refused to exploit his divine status for his own advantage. When Christ "emptied himself" (2:7), he did not cease to be divine. Rather, he gave up the "form" of God and took up the form of a slave by becoming human. In becoming human and accepting death on the cross (2:8) Jesus proved himself the perfect example of humility and obedience—an example that his followers should take seriously (see 2:5).

In the second stanza (2:9-11) Jesus' resurrection is taken as a part or a moment in the larger process of God's exaltation of Jesus (2:9). The "name that is above every name" is "Lord" (*Kyrios* in Greek), the title applied in the Greek version of the Old Testament to Yahweh, the God of Israel. This text helps to explain how the title "Lord" could be applied to Jesus in early Christian circles (see 2:11 below) without destroying Jewish and Christian belief in the oneness of God: God gave that name Lord/*Kyrios* at his exaltation. Because the name of Jesus is now connected with Lord (see 2:9, 11), all creatures in the universe must do him homage. For the images of the bended knee and the confessing tongue in 2:10, see Isaiah 45:23 (Septuagint). In 2:11 the hymn reaches its climax with a reference to an already existing (see Rom 10:9; 1 Cor 12:3) summary of Christian faith: "Jesus Christ is Lord." In fact, this summary may well have been the starting point of the hymn, which explains why and how Jesus can be celebrated as Lord. The final phrase "to the glory of God the Father" explains the goal or purpose of the entire process described in the hymn. The proclamation and acknowledgment of God's glory are the "end" of Christ's humiliation and exaltation (see Rom 6:10-11; 1 Cor 15:28).

The hymn celebrating Christ the Servant in 2:6-11 is also theologically controversial. The major matters of controversy appear near the start of the hymn, due largely to the vocabulary used in 2:6-7. The chief questions are: What is being said about Christ Jesus? Did he exist in another form before he became human? Was he divine? Did he set aside or "turn off" his divinity in becoming human?

The most common approach to these questions is to assume that according to the early Christian hymn preserved in 2:6-11 Christ Jesus existed as a divine being before he became human (2:6) and now enjoys the status of "Lord" (2:9-11). Rather than setting aside or turning off his divine status, he simply refused to use it for his own advantage. Instead, he humbled himself first by becoming human and then by his death on the cross.

Another reading finds no reference in 2:6 to Christ's divinity or pre-existence. It sees only Jesus of Nazareth as a human being under discussion and finds an allusion to him as the second and better Adam. Whereas the first Adam was created in the image of God (see Gn 1:26-27) and sought to be "like God" (Gn 3:5), the second and better Adam (see Rom 5:12-21) refused to exploit being in the image of God but rather emptied and humbled himself. Proponents of this approach discern allusions in the hymn to the Suffering Servant of Isaiah 53 and to the Suffering Righteous One of Wisdom 2–3.

The controversies about the literary outline and christological claims of 2:6-11 should not deflect attention from what the text says clearly. It celebrates the lordship of Christ over all creation and relates that lordship to his death. As a very early witness to Christian beliefs about Christ, it provides a theological context for understanding what Christians meant by the confession "Jesus Christ is Lord" (2:11).

How did this hymn contribute to Paul's argument in his letter to the Philippians? The introduction in 2:5 indicates that Paul regarded it as proof or substantiation for his exhortation to mutual respect and humility. The key phrase for Paul was probably "he humbled himself" (2:8), since the hymn is used to encourage an attitude of "humbly regard[ing] others as more important than yourselves" (2:3). Thus Paul used a christological confession of extraordinary richness to strengthen an appeal to better behavior by calling on the example of Christ Jesus the Lord.

Further Instructions (2:12-18)

¹²So then, my beloved, obedient as you have always been, not only when I am present but all the more now when I am absent, work out your salvation with fear and trembling. ¹³For God is the one who, for his good purpose, works in you both to desire and to work.

¹⁴Do everything without grumbling or questioning, ¹⁵that you may be blameless and innocent, children of God without blemish in the midst of a crooked and perverse generation, among whom you shine like lights in the world, ¹⁶as you hold on to the word of life, so that my boast for the day of Christ may be that I did not run in vain or labor in vain. ¹⁷But, even as I am poured out as a libation upon the sacrificial service of your faith, I rejoice and share my joy with all of you. ¹⁸In the same way you also should rejoice and share your joy with me.

Having urged the Philippians to union of hearts and minds in 1:27–2:4 and having appealed to the example of Christ Jesus in 2:5-11, Paul presents a general exhortation in 2:12-13 and a more concrete exhortation in 2:14-18.

The general exhortation (2:12-13) is directed to the Philippians to work out their salvation "with fear and trembling" (see 1 Cor 2:3; 2 Cor 7:15; Eph 6:5). The expression refers not so much to a servile or fearful attitude toward God but rather to the hostile circumstances and the hard challenges that Christians face in their everyday lives. The emphasis on the

Christian's contribution to salvation is balanced by the typically Pauline emphasis on God's initiative in the process of salvation: "God is the one who ... works in you" (2:13). Paul leaves no opening for those who might seek to construct their own salvation and acquire it by their human efforts alone. God is the ultimate source of all the human desires and actions that please God.

The more concrete exhortation (2:14-18) attacks directly the divisions alluded to in 1:27–2:4. The references to "grumbling or questioning" in 2:14 and to a "crooked and perverse generation" in 2:15 take ancient Israel's murmuring in the wilderness (Ex 16) and its twisted behavior (see Dt 32:5) as negative examples to be avoided (as in Heb 3–4). The positive advice for the Philippians is that they should be faithful to their call to be "lights in the world" (2:15; see Dn 12:3; Mt 5:14-16) and to hold fast to the gospel or "word of life" (2:16).

As a transition between 1:27–2:18 and 2:19-30 Paul appeals in 2:16-18 to his own situation. At the day of Christ's second coming, Paul wants to be able to point with justifiable pride to his apostolic labors among the Philippians (2:16b). But even if he were to be killed for preaching the gospel of Christ, he views that death as a cause for joy—both for himself and for other Christians (2:17-18). In talking about the possibility of his death, Paul uses words associated with worship ("poured out as a libation upon the sacrificial service of your faith") that together suggest a sacrifical dimension to his impending death if things were to turn out differently from what he imagined in 1:24-26. A "libation" was a drink-offering poured out to God (or to the gods). A "sacrificial service" (or "liturgy") was a service performed by someone for the state or the people (see Rom 15:16; Phil 2:30). In both 2:17 and 2:18 Paul uses words for "joy" that express his personal joy and the joy that he asks the Philippians to arouse on his behalf.

Travel Plans (2:19–3:1)

¹⁹I hope, in the Lord Jesus, to send Timothy to you soon, so that I too may be heartened by hearing news of you. ²⁰For I have no one comparable to him for genuine interest in whatever concerns you. ²¹For they all seek their own interests, not those of Jesus Christ. ²²But you know his worth, how as a child with a father he served along with me in the cause of the gospel. ²³He it is, then, whom I hope to send as soon as I see how things go with me, ²⁴but I am confident in the Lord that I myself will also come soon.

²⁵With regard to Epaphroditus, my brother and co-worker and fellow soldier, your messenger and minister in my need, I consider it necessary to send him to you. ²⁶For he has been longing for all of you and was distressed because you heard that he was ill. ²⁷He was indeed ill, close to death; but God had mercy on him, not just on him but also on me, so that I might not have sorrow upon sorrow. ²⁸I send him therefore with the greater eagerness, so that, on seeing him, you may rejoice again, and I may have less anxiety. ²⁹Welcome him then in the Lord with all joy and hold such people in esteem, ³⁰because for the sake of the work of Christ he came close to death, risking his life to make up for those services to me that you could not perform.

^{3:1}Finally, my brothers, rejoice in the Lord.

Since Paul is in prison and his future is still in doubt, he has no clear travel plans for himself. Instead, he talks about the travel plans of his two co-workers, Timothy

(2:19-24) and Epaphroditus (2:25-30), and issues another call to rejoice (3:1a). Paul's hope is that he himself will be able to visit the Philippians (2:24). When he learns his fate and things are resolved, he intends to send Timothy to the Philippians. In the meantime, he plans to send Epaphroditus, perhaps along with the present letter. The amount of communication and traveling implied by these plans is another reason for placing the composition of the letter in a place fairly close to Philippi (Ephesus) rather than Caesarea Maritima or Rome.

Paul uses the verb "I hope" in connection with his travel plans elsewhere (see Phlm 22; 1 Cor 16:7; Rom 15:24). Timothy was mentioned in 1:1 along with Paul as co-author of the letter. But the rest of the letter has been written in the first-person singular, indicating Paul as the principal author. In 2:19-24 Paul presents Timothy as knowing what Paul himself would do or say in a given situation and therefore as an appropriate spokesman for him (see 1 Cor 16:10-11). Here Timothy is commended as sharing Paul's very "soul," as concerned with the affairs of the Philippians, as dedicated to Christ, as like a son to Paul, and as a servant of the gospel. The criticism of the other co-workers in 2:21 ("they all seek their own interests, not those of Jesus Christ") is clearly an exaggeration, since Epaphroditus and presumably others would not be included in their number. Nevertheless, the remark betrays a certain frustration and isolation on Paul's part. Again in 2:23-24 Paul expresses confidence that he will be released and allowed to work again among the Philippian Christians. But the fact that Paul brings this matter up so often in this short letter (see 1:12, 19-20, 25-26; 2:17-18, 23-24) leads one to question how confident he really was.

According to 4:18, Epaphroditus brought the Philippians' gift to Paul. Thus Paul describes him as "your messenger and minister in my need" (2:25). The other titles applied to him ("my brother and co-worker and fellow soldier") stress his involvement in Paul's apostolic activity. He may be the same as the Epaphras who is mentioned in the letters to Philemon and the Colossians. After praising Epaphroditus' service to the gospel and to the Philippians (2:25), Paul mentions the news of Epaphroditus' serious illness in 2:26-27, and gives thanks to God that he has now returned to good health and so can fulfill his mission on Paul's behalf to the Philippians. By instructing his readers to welcome Epaphroditus "with all joy" (2:29) Paul returns to a principal theme of the letter (see 1:4, 18, 25; 2:2, 17-18) and prepares for 3:1a ("rejoice in the Lord"). The expression "to make up for those services to me that you could not perform" in 2:30 may allude to the gift conveyed by Epaphroditus to Paul from the Philippians (see 4:18). It need not be taken as a criticism of them.

Paul's "travel plans" (usually at the end of his letters) remind us that he did not set out to write theological treatises. Though there is much theology in his letters, there is also information about projected visits and all kinds of other activities. Early Christianity spread through the Mediterranean world in the mid-first century mainly by a network of traveling missionaries and the communities that received them. The written documents that we possess were regarded at best as weak substitutes for the personal presence of the apostles.

Paul's Transformation (3:1b-11)

[1b]Writing the same things to you is no burden for me but is a safeguard for you. [2]Beware of the dogs! Beware of

the evil-workers! Beware of the mutilation! [3]For we are the circumcision, we who worship through the Spirit of God, who boast in Christ Jesus and do not put our confidence in flesh, [4]although I myself have grounds for confidence even in the flesh. If anyone else thinks he can be confident in the flesh, all the more can I. [5]Circumcised on the eighth day, of the race of Israel, of the tribe of Benjamin, a Hebrew of Hebrew parentage, in observance of the law a Pharisee, [6]in zeal I persecuted the church, in righteousness based on the law I was blameless.

[7][But] whatever gains I had, these I have come to consider a loss because of Christ. [8]More than that, I even consider everything as a loss because of the supreme good of knowing Christ Jesus my Lord. For his sake I have accepted the loss of all things and I consider them to be so much rubbish, that I may gain Christ [9]and be found in him, not having any righteousness of my own based on the law but that which comes through faith in Christ, the righteousness from God, depending on faith, [10]to know him and the power of his resurrection and [the] sharing of his sufferings by being conformed to his death, [11]if somehow I may attain the resurrection from the dead.

Chapter 3 probably originated separately from chapters 1 and 2, and was joined to them at some stage in the editorial process (see the discussion of this matter in the introduction to Philippians). There is no indication in chapter 3 that Paul is a prisoner, even though appeal to his imprisonment might have added to Paul's qualifications as a Christian and might explain why (because of his physical absence) the Philippians needed especially to be on guard against what Paul regarded as a false gospel. Many interpreters assume that Paul had already been released from prison and wrote this letter after the main letter (1:1–3:1a) to advise the Philippian Christians as they faced a new crisis.

The second part of 3:1 ("writing the same things ...") more likely refers to what follows rather than to what preceded. Paul wishes to guard the spiritual security of those who are addressed by warning them against false teachers. In 3:2 the tone changes from encouragement of the Philippians to attack against opponents of Paul's gospel. Paul seems to address a specific problem at Philippi: the appearance of Jewish Christian missionaries there, who insisted that the Gentile Christians must live and act as Jews by undergoing circumcision and observing the works of the Mosaic Law. Paul dealt with similar problems in 2 Corinthians 10–13 and Galatians.

After explaining that he writes to bolster the faith of the Philippian Christians (3:1b), Paul in 3:2-3 attacks the Jewish Christian missionaries in a vigorous manner. By referring to them as "dogs" ("Beware of the dogs!") Paul throws back at them their own contemptuous way of talking about non-Jews (see Mt 15:26-27). By calling them "evil-workers" Paul alludes to their insistence of the "works of the Law." By using the term "mutilation" Paul alludes to their insistence that Gentile Christians undergo circumcision. Then in 3:3 Paul associates himself with the Gentile Christians of Philippi as constituting the "true circumcision." Against the claims of the Jewish Christians Paul denies the need for physical circumcision and transfers its role in marking the people of God to those who worship in/by the Spirit of God, boast in Christ Jesus, and do not put their trust in the flesh. For similar claims see Romans 2:27-29; 4:11-12; Galatians 6:12-13; Colossians 2:11.

With an eye toward the Jewish Christian missionaries, Paul in 3:4-6 lists his qualifications as a Jew with regard to his birth and his religious achievements. Since circumcision pertains to the flesh, Paul argues that insistence on it is to put confidence in the flesh. But for Paul "flesh" is the opposite of "spirit," and those who trust in the flesh are not on God's side.

Nevertheless, he is prepared to match his qualifications "in the flesh" with any other Jew or Jewish Christian. Paul claims in 3:5 to have been "circumcised on the eighth day" in accord with strict Jewish law regarding the time between birth and circumcision (see Gn 17:12; 21:4; Lv 12:3; Lk 1:59). The other qualifications associated with Paul's birth—Israelite, Hebrew, Benjaminite—strengthen Paul's identity as a Jew, perhaps in answer to criticisms that he had been born in Tarsus of Cilicia—outside of the land of Israel. Paul uses his membership in the Pharisees as a badge of honor in establishing his Jewishness. He claims to have followed faithfully the traditions of the Pharisees in interpreting and living the Mosaic Law. Though identified as a Pharisee in Acts 23:6 and 26:5, nowhere else does Paul himself claim to have been a Pharisee. See Galatians 1:14 for another statement about Paul's life in Judaism.

According to 3:6 Paul's zeal for the Law as a Pharisee led him to persecute the Church (see also Gal 1:3; Acts 8:3). By describing himself as "blameless" Paul indicates that he felt no guilt about failing to observe the Law or about persecuting the Church.

Having established his credentials as a Jew, Paul in 3:7-11 describes his transformation "in Christ." Using "profit and loss" terminology (see also 4:15-18; Phlm 17-20), Paul in 3:7-8 bears witness to the change of values that occurred with his coming to know Christ. What he had regarded as profitable "in the flesh" (in his Jewish birth and his advancement within Judaism), he came to consider of no real value. With his new relationship with God through Christ Jesus, Paul underwent a "transvaluation" or change of values: What had been important was no longer, and what he had persecuted became what he embraced. With the term "rubbish" (a very strong word) Paul contrasts his privileges and achievements in the past with the surpassing value of knowing Christ. What it means to "gain Christ" (3:8) is spelled out in the following verses: being found in Christ, getting genuine righteousness, and sharing in Christ's death and resurrection.

In 3:9-11 Paul explains what he expects to get from knowing Christ: righteousness now before God, and eternal life in the resurrection of the dead. The fidelity shown by Christ to the Father, and not the Mosaic Law, is the source of Paul's own right relationship with God. Knowing Christ means identification with his death and resurrection, and thus sharing his suffering and its rewards. This knowledge of Christ (see 3:8, 10) has replaced whatever value Paul had previously placed on his birth and achievements in Judaism. The most important term in 3:10 to express Paul's relationship with God through Christ is "being conformed to his death." Paul has taken on the "form" of Christ (see 2:6). In 3:11 as elsewhere (see Rom 6:8) Paul insists that the fullness of resurrected life lies in the future and the Christian must carry on as a pilgrim toward it. For the idea that the resurrection is already past, see 2 Timothy 2:18, where that view is vigorously refuted.

There has been a lively debate among New Testament scholars whether it is proper to call Paul a "convert." The resolution of the debate depends to a large extent on how one defines "convert." If conversion means moving from one religion to another, Paul was not a convert from Judaism to Christianity, since the two were probably not yet perceived as two different religions, and since in Paul's eyes and in the eyes of at least some others he remained a Jew. If conversion applies to moving from one kind of Judaism (Pharisaism) to another (Christianity), Paul was a convert. What was most important and decisive for Paul was his being "conformed" to Christ through baptism into his death in the hope of sharing his resurrection (see Rom 6:1-11). This experience transformed Paul's way of thinking and his manner of acting.

It is important to recognize the polemical situation of Paul's remarks in Philippians 3. His opponents are Jewish Christians who insist that Gentile Christians must become Jews in order to be real Christians. As the apostle to the Gentiles, Paul was convinced that Gentiles did not have to go through Judaism in order to become part of the people of God. Here Paul calls upon his own positive experience of being "conformed" to Christ to argue that even the best Jewish credentials are insignificant in comparison with the "supreme good of knowing Christ Jesus my Lord" (3:8).

Paul the Pharisee had sought right relationship ("justification") with God in the Mosaic Law (3:6). Paul the Christian found right relation with God in Christ's death and resurrection (3:9-11). With this discovery he came to recognize that faith or fidelity—Christ's fidelity to the Father, our participation in that fidelity—is the sphere in which right relationship with God is to be found. This theological recognition provided the basis for Paul's insisting that Gentile Christians need not be forced to go through Judaism in order to become full Christians. Being "conformed" to Christ, not the works of the Law, is the way to the righteousness that comes from God.

Present Struggle and Future Hope (3:12—4:1)

¹²It is not that I have already taken hold of it or have already attained perfect maturity, but I continue my pursuit in hope that I may possess it, since I have indeed been taken possession of by Christ [Jesus]. ¹³Brothers, I for my part do not consider myself to have taken possession. Just one thing: forgetting what lies behind and straining forward to what lies ahead, ¹⁴I continue my pursuit toward the goal, the prize of God's upward calling, in Christ Jesus. ¹⁵Let us, then, who are "perfectly mature" adopt this attitude. And if you have a different atttitude, this too God will reveal to you. ¹⁶Only, with regard to what we have attained, continue on the same course.

¹⁷Join with others in being imitators of me, brothers, and observe those who thus conduct themselves according to the model you have in us. ¹⁸For many, as I have often told you and now tell you even in tears, conduct themselves as enemies of the cross of Christ. ¹⁹Their end is destruction. Their God is their stomach; their glory is in their "shame." Their minds are occupied with earthly things. ²⁰But our citizenship is in heaven, and from it we also await a savior, the Lord Jesus Christ. ²¹He will change our lowly body to conform with his glorified body by the power that enables him also to bring all things into subjection to himself.

⁴:¹Therefore, my brothers, whom I love and long for, my joy and crown, in this way stand firm in the Lord, beloved.

The first part (3:12-16) of this section reflects on the incompleteness of Christian life in the present (the "not yet" dimension of the kingdom) and the struggle involved in holding on to what has already been attained. Paul's statements in 3:12-14 revolve around the words "attain/possess" and "pursue." What Paul had not yet taken hold of (3:12) is either the resurrection from the dead in particular (3:11) or everything mentioned in 3:9-11. The verb "take hold" occurs three times in 3:12-13 and expresses also Paul's experience of having first been taken hold of by Christ. In the course of describing the activity demanded of the Christian, Paul insists first on the initiative of Christ in Christian life ("I have indeed been taken possession of by Christ Jesus," 3:12). The idea of "perfect maturity" in 3:12 prepares for reference to the "perfectly mature" in 3:15.

The struggle involved in Christian life in the present is expressed in 3:13-14 (and perhaps even in 3:12) with the help of various athletic images ("straining forward ... pursuit ... goal ... prize"). Some interpreters find in the expression "the prize of God's upward calling in Christ Jesus" (3:14) the idea of a winner being called up publicly to receive the prize after an athletic contest. The point here is that Christian life moves toward its goal of being called up to the fullness of the divine life with Christ Jesus. For the metaphor of Christian life as a race, see 1 Corinthians 9:24 and 2 Timothy 4:7.

Even though in 3:12 Paul said that he had not yet attained "perfect maturity," in 3:15 he associates himself (perhaps with some irony) with the "perfectly mature." His opponents may have claimed that they were "perfect." In 3:5-6 Paul had shown that he could match the credentials of perfection with anyone. Perhaps also the opponents appealed to revelations that they had received—which might explain the reference to revelation in 3:15. The exhortation to "continue on the same course" in 3:16 fits with Paul's frequent summons to unity of hearts and minds (as in 2:2, 5) and to holding firm to the gospel that the Philippians had been taught.

The second part (3:17-21) reflects on the promise of fullness of life in and with Christ Jesus. Paul first in 3:17 urges the Philippians to be "imitators" of him insofar as he has been "conformed" to Christ (see 3:10). He wishes others to imitate him in imitating Christ (see 2:6-11). The goal is total conformity to Christ. That means allowing Christ to shape the Christian and welcoming Christ to take shape in oneself so that the Christian shares the same "form" as Christ ("he was in the form of God," 2:6). This powerful image of "conformity" to Christ is at the root of Paul's understanding of conversion as a transformation into the death and resurrection of Christ. It is what is meant when one speaks of Pauline mysticism—an absorption into Christ's death and resurrection as well as a willingness to let that central mystery shine forth in one's life: "Yet I live, no longer I, but Christ lives in me" (Gal 2:20).

In 3:18-19 Paul warns against the "enemies of the cross." The opponents apparently fail to recognize the newness of the cross (in contrast to the Law), its power as the sign of God's wisdom (though apparently foolishness), and its function in reconciling Jews and Gentiles in Christ. Insofar as they have failed to grasp the theological reality underlying Paul's gospel, they are enemies of the cross. Their end is destruction at the final judgment. At that judgment what they imagine is their glory will turn out to be their shame. The charge that "their God is their stomach" most likely refers to the emphasis that the opponents placed on observance of the Jewish food laws.

Were the opponents in 3:18-19 the same as those in 3:2? And were they Christians? Although it may be hard for us today to imagine that Paul would call other Jewish Christians "enemies of the cross" as he does in 3:18, the most straightforward reading of the text assumes that the opponents remain the same. They were apparently Jewish Christians who insisted that Gentile Christians be circumcised and obey the Jewish dietary and Sabbath laws. Paul dismisses their program in 3:19 as concerned with "earthly things."

The warning against the opponents is balanced by a promise to those who imitate Paul's example and become "conformed" to Christ (3:20-21). In contrast to those who are concerned with "earthly things" Paul proclaims that "our citizenship" is in heaven. Philippi was a Roman colony, and its people would have been sensitive to such political imagery. But Paul's emphasis is not on the Philippian church as God's colony on earth, but rather on the true blessings that Christians can expect from their heavenly home. In the end (3:21) the process of transformation that began in sharing Christ's death in baptism and living in "conformity" with Christ will reach its fullness in sharing in Christ's resurrection and glorification ("with his glorified body"). The idea that God will subject all things to Christ is developed more fully in 1 Corinthians 15:27-28. Here it is appealed to as the ground for the transformation and "conformation" that will take place in the case of those who await Christ as savior from heaven and share in the fullness of his glory. Some interpreters find in

3:20-21 verbal links with the hymn in 2:6-11, especially in the language of "form" (2:7; 3:21) and the theme of glory (2:11; 3:21).

The section ends in 4:1 with a passionate plea ("my brothers whom I love and long for, my joy and crown") for the Philippians to stand firm in the Lord. If Philippians 3 contains the bulk of a letter sent by Paul to the Philippians after his release from prison (as is suggested by the lack of reference to his imprisonment and the stronger tone taken against the opponents in 3:2 and 3:18-19), where does this letter end? Some commentators end this letter at 4:1. Others regard 4:8-9 as the continuation of 4:1. Still others include 4:2-3 and/or 4:4-7 in this letter. Rather than taking a firm decision about this matter and cutting up the sequence of the text as we now have it, we will treat 4:2-9 together in the next section. It should be noted, however, that those who place 4:2-3 with Philippians 3 make Euodia and Syntyche into the instigators or occasions of the troubles addressed in this letter, though there is no other indication that the opponents included women among their leaders.

Exhortations (4:2-9)

> ²I urge Euodia and I urge Syntyche to come to a mutual understanding in the Lord. ³Yes, and I ask you also, my true yokemate, to help them, for they have struggled at my side in promoting the gospel, along with Clement and my other co-workers, whose names are in the book of life.
> ⁴Rejoice in the Lord always. I shall say it again: rejoice! ⁵Your kindness should be known to all. The Lord is near. ⁶Have no anxiety at all, but in everything, by prayer and petition, with thanksgiving, make your requests known to

God. [7]Then the peace of God that surpasses all understanding will guard your hearts and minds in Christ Jesus.

[8]Finally, brothers, whatever is true, whatever is honorable, whatever is just, whatever is pure, whatever is lovely, whatever is gracious, if there is any excellence and if there is anything worthy of praise, think about these things. [9]Keep on doing what you have learned and received and heard and seen in me. Then the God of peace will be with you.

The first part (4:2-3) is Paul's exhortation to two women—Euodia and Syntyche—to agree "in the Lord" and to someone else known either by the proper name (otherwise unattested) Syzygos or by a nickname "yoke-mate" (for close "co-worker," based on the image of two beasts of burden attached to the same "yoke"). The exhortation for Euodia and Syntyche to come to a mutual understanding and the repetiton of "I urge" suggests a serious disagreement between them. But the precise issue and how the matter was resolved are not clear. Clement was a common name in the Roman world, though there may be some connection with the Clement who later became the bishop of Rome (see his letter to the Corinthians known as 1 Clement). The verb "struggled" and the syntax ("my other co-workers") suggest that Euodia and Syntyche were numbered among Paul's co-workers. The image of the "book of life" containing the names of the blessed ones appears in the Old Testament (Ex 32:32; Dn 12:1; Pss 69:29; 139:16) and the New Testament (Lk 10:20; Rv 3:5; 20:15; 21:27).

If 4:2-3 continues 3:1–4:1, then the impression is given that the two women had a role in the spread of the teaching under criticism there—perhaps at least by allowing the Jewish Christian missionaries to use their house(s) as a gathering place. But there is no direct reference to that in 4:2-3, where the cause of the quarrel between the two is left unspecified. On the other hand, 4:2-3 flows more smoothly from the directions and news about persons presented in 2:19-30. Thus the change of subject and of tone ("I urge") constitutes another argument for taking 3:1b–4:1 as a separate letter and for viewing 4:2-3 as the continuation of the main letter.

The second part (4:4-7) consists of general exhortations and wishes expressed in various grammatical forms: imperatives, subjunctives, indicatives, and so forth. The repetition of "rejoice" and the surrounding words ("always ... again") underscore the importance of a prominent theme in the letter (see 1:18; 2:17-18, 28; 3:1; 4:10). The basis for Christian joy is being "in the Lord." Besides joy in the Lord, Paul recommends gentleness in dealing with others, unceasing prayer, and trust in God's power to give peace. The term translated "kindness" in 4:5 conveys the idea of gentleness, graciousness, and forbearance to others, not trying to display superiority or power over others (see 2:1-5). The statement that the Lord is near (4:5) is usually taken in the temporal sense that Jesus' second coming is near (see Rom 13:11-12). The idea that the Lord's presence among us means that he is always near is less appropriate. The piling up of words for prayer in 4:6 ("prayer ... petition ... thanksgiving ... requests") makes the point of continuous prayer: pray and pray and pray. It is unlikely that "thanksgiving" here refers directly to the eucharist. In 4:7 it is assumed that God is the origin and content of genuine peace, and that God's peace transcends human calculations and plans.

The third part (4:8-9) urges the Philippians to think about (that is, concentrate on, put their energy into) what is virtuous and praiseworthy (4:8) and to practice what they have learned from Paul (4:9). As in 4:7 above, God is the origin and basis of genuine peace. (For the "God of peace," see Rom 15:33; 16:20; 1 Cor 14:33; 2 Cor 13:11; and 1 Thes 2:15.)

The topics of the three parts of this section—instructions to individuals (4:2-3), exhortations related to behavior (4:4-7), and virtues to be pursued (4:8-9)—are familiar from the other Pauline letters. But in Philippians their connections are especially awkward, and so they are better taken as pearls on a string and treasured for what they each contribute to Paul's message rather than as forming a tight unit.

Paul's Thank-You Note (4:10-20)

[10] I rejoice greatly in the Lord that now at last you revived your concern for me. You were, of course, concerned about me but lacked an opportunity. [11] Not that I say this because of need, for I have learned, in whatever situation I find myself, to be self-sufficient. [12] I know indeed how to live in humble circumstances; I know also how to live with abundance. In every circumstance and in all things I have learned the secret of being well fed and of going hungry, of living in abundance and of being in need. [13] I have the strength for everything through him who empowers me.

[14] Still it was kind of you to share in my distress. [15] You Philippians indeed know that at the beginning of the gospel, when I left Macedonia, not a single church shared with me in an account of giving and receiving, except you alone. [16] For even when I was at Thessalonica

you sent me something for my needs, not only once but more than once. [17] It is not that I am eager for the gift; rather, I am eager for the profit that accrues to your account. [18] I have received full payment and I abound. I am very well supplied because of what I received from you through Epaphroditus, "a fragrant aroma," an acceptable sacrifice, pleasing to God. [19] My God will fully supply whatever you need, in accord with his glorious riches in Christ Jesus. [20] To our God and Father, glory forever and ever. Amen.

It is likely that what is now 4:10-20 was a separate letter, written before the other parts of Philippians and joined to them in the process of collecting Paul's correspondence with the Philippian Christians. Though Paul speaks of his "distress" in 4:14, it is not certain that he is yet a prisoner. Moreover, it seems ungracious that Paul would have postponed his expression of thanks to the Philippians for their gift to so late in the letter if 4:10-20 is now in its original place. Also the beginning ("I rejoice greatly") needs only the customary salutation to be taken as the start of a letter and the doxology at the end ("To our God and Father, glory ...") rounds off the text. That 4:10-20 shares certain terms and ideas with the main letter ("rejoice ... your concern") does not refute this theory, since Paul was writing in the same basic situation to the same group of people and so used some of the same words. If not originally a separate letter, 4:10-20 is at least a self-contained unit.

The "thank-you" note begins with Paul's expression of joy over the fact that the Philippians have shown their concern for him through a gift (4:10). Paul's joy is "in the Lord" because by their gift the Philippians are cooperating in the spreading of the gospel. The expression "now at last" need not be interpreted negatively as a criticism of the Philippians' slowness to act on Paul's behalf. In fact, Paul goes on to admit that the Philippians had no opportunity to help him either because the circumstances did not allow it or because of Paul's own policy of self-sufficiency.

Then in 4:11-13 Paul denies that he really needed the gift, since he has learned to be self-sufficient whatever the circumstances. The term "self-sufficient" (4:11) expressed an important virtue for contemporary philosophers, especially Stoics and Cynics. For Paul, however, self-sufficiency was not merely a philosophical virtue. Its basis was in the one "who empowers me" (4:13), and its exercise was in the service of the gospel. It allowed Paul to labor effectively for the gospel even in the face of great obstacles (4:12; for other catalogues of Paul's apostolic sufferings, see 1 Cor 4:11-13; 2 Cor 6:3-10; 11:23-29). Paul could put up with anything, because the Lord strengthened him (4:13).

Next, Paul praises the Philippians for sharing his "distress" (4:14) and recalls their past benefactions to him (4:15-16). Paul does not specify what the distress was. It need not have been his imprisoment. It may well have been the circumstances that led to his imprisonment. At any rate Paul commends the Philippians for their gift and takes it as the occasion to develop the idea that their gift is a way of sharing in the gospel mission. The expression "the beginning of the gospel" in 4:15 apparently refers to Paul's activity in preaching the gospel in Europe. He goes on to allude to the difficulties that he faced when he came to Corinth (see 2 Cor 11:8-9). The Philippians gave him the necessary aid. In Paul's correspondence with the Thessalonians there is no mention of the aid referred to in 4:16. Perhaps Paul wished not to embarrass the Thessalonians. Perhaps the Philippians' aid met only part of his need there.

Then in 4:17-18 Paul reflects on the significance of the Philippians' gift to him first in financial terms and then in terms of sacrifice. The Philippians' gift associates them more concretely and closely with Paul's mission and thus adds to their "account" that is to be totalled up at the last judgment when the "profit" (literally, "fruit" understood figuratively) of one's activity will be made manifest. In 4:18 Paul continues the financial terminology ("I have received full payment"). Indeed, the Philippians' gift through Epaphroditus has been received by him as more than full payment. Of course, the real recipient of the gift is God, as the sacrificial imagery that follows makes clear. The "fragrant aroma" alludes to the use of incense in connection with sacrifices.

Paul concludes with a prayer on the Philippians' behalf (4:19) and a doxology (4:20). The qualifying phrase "in Christ Jesus" in 4:19 reasserts the pivotal importance of Christ in our relations with God. The doxology ("To our God and Father, glory ...") is a fitting conclusion. There is no verb in the sentence. If one supplies "be," it is a wish that all creation acknowledge the glory of God. If one supplies "is," it is a statement acknowledging the eternal glory that is God's. The term "Amen" ("I/we believe it") seals the prayer and doxology.

This passage is noteworthy for its Christian uses of technical terms and metaphors. First, in 4:11 Paul declares himself to be "self-sufficient" with a term well known from contemporary philosophy but transformed by the claim that Paul's sufficiency is not really from himself but rather from God who empowers him (4:13). Then, in 4:17-18a (as in Phlm 17-20) Paul uses financial imagery to express the transaction between the Philippians and himself. Finally, in 4:18b he uses the language of sacrifice and temple worship to interpret the Philippians' gift as given in the last analysis to God.

In 4:10-20 we can discern a certain tension between Paul's policy of independence and his affection for what the Philippian Christians have done by their gift. But we are not sure of Paul's tone. Is he annoyed (because he feels abandoned)? Or is he embarrassed (because he wants to preserve his independence)? Or is he ambivalent (because he is torn between his principles and his affection for the Philippians)? Or is he pleased (because in his time of need his old friends have come to his aid)? Or is he all four at once? All we have now in 4:10-20 are words on page. There is no way of discerning the verbal nuances or bodily gestures behind Paul's words. The Philippians at least had experienced Paul in person and presumably that would have helped them in being sensitive to Paul's tone and nuances.

Indeed, we are not even sure of the precise nature of the gift, though the financial imagery of 4:17-18a suggests that it was money. Perhaps it was intended to help Paul buy himself out of prison or out of the proceedings that would result in his imprisonment. Such transactions were common and easy at that time. In any case, the gift revives and strengthens the longstanding relationship between Paul and his Philippian converts to Christianity. Paul takes the occasion of their gift to him to renew a friendship "in the Lord."

Final Greetings (4:21-23)

> ²¹ Give my greetings to every holy one in Christ Jesus. The brothers who are with me send you their greetings; ²² all the holy ones send you their greetings, especially those of Caesar's household. ²³ The grace of the Lord Jesus Christ be with your spirit.

The letter ends with personal greetings (4:21-22) and a final prayer (4:23). Both are standard features in Paul's letters. (For other final greetings, see Rom 16:3-16, 21-23; 1 Cor 16:19-20; 2 Cor 13:11-13; 1 Thes 5:26; and Phlm 23-24. For other final prayers, see Rom 16:20; 1 Cor 16:23-24; 2 Cor 13:14; Gal 6:18; 1 Thes 5:28; and Phlm 25.) While formulaic, these greetings and prayers bear witness to the close bonds existing among those who are "in Christ Jesus."

Here as elsewhere in Paul's letters, "holy one" or "saint" is a way of referring to other Christians. Their holiness derives from God the Holy One and resides (as they do) in Christ Jesus. The reference to "Caesar's household" in 4:22 need not be taken as proof that Paul wrote from Rome. The expression can also refer to those who performed administrative tasks for the Roman empire, especially in its important cities.

Philippians in Christian Life

Imaginative Recreation: Before focusing on important themes in Paul's letter to the Philippians, it may be helpful to look at the text from the imaginative perspective of a Philippian Christian. Imagine that you were brought to Christian faith by Paul himself. You recall clearly his explanations of the good news about Jesus and about the possibility of a new relationship with God through Jesus. Despite Paul's weak bodily presence and his failure to impress as a speaker (see 2 Cor 10:10), Paul had an impact on you as no other human being ever had. You turned from your civic religion and your pagan cult to the church of Jesus Christ. And you found wisdom and joy there, and a new family too. But then Paul went away to continue his mission of founding new churches. And problems arose in Philippi. Imagine yourself as part of the community that receives Paul's letters in their (hypothetical) chronological sequence.

The first news we received from Paul by letter (4:10-20) puzzled us. We had contributed to a collection of money that could be used to help Paul to buy his way out of the trouble he was in. But at first Paul sounds testy. He says that "now at last" we have done something, and that he really does not need the gift. But then he warms up by recalling our prior generosity and by affirming that our gift really goes to God (who will surely reward us). Paul is a complex person!

Sometime later a longer letter (1:1–3:1a; 4:2-9, 21-23) arrives. Now Paul is in prison and soon will go on trial. We are very worried about him. And yet Paul is fully convinced that no matter what happens everything will turn out for the good. In fact, he sees in his imprisonment the occasion for an even more successful spreading of the gospel. But Paul has something else on his mind—the divisions and conflicts in our community. He wants us to work harder at unity—at listening, understanding, and respecting one another in Christ Jesus. He wants us to follow the example of Christ the Servant who died for us.

And he is so concerned about us that he is going to send Timothy and Epaphroditus to help us to resolve our problems.

Still later a third letter (3:1b–4:1) arrives. This is strong stuff! But we need it. Those Jewish Christian missionaries are causing a lot of trouble for us. They say we have to become Jews, to get circumcised and to observe the food laws and Sabbath regulations. They say that Paul is not a good Jew. Did Paul tell them! He matched qualifications in Judaism with them—and more. Then he said that what is more important is our taking on the "form" of Christ, being formed by Christ and being "conformed" to him. That is what makes us Gentiles part of God's people. We don't have to become Jews to do it.

These letters are very helpful. They address our problems, and Paul really knows us. Someone should put them together in a collection so they don't get lost!

Points for Meditation: The most important theological contribution of Paul's letter to the Philippians is undoubtedly the hymn preserved in 2:6-11. It shows that at a very early time in Christian history Christ Jesus was celebrated as sharing the "form" of God and as worthy of the divine title "Lord." It also stresses his humanity in emptying himself not only in his birth but also (and especially) in his suffering and death on the cross.

This hymn is the starting point for the letter's most profound contribution to understanding Christian life as being "formed" by Christ and participating in his life. Paul's "self-sufficiency" and his ability to face suffering and even death without fear flow from his conviction that through his sharing in Christ's life for him (and for us) eternal life has already begun. Nothing can take that away.

The joy and peace that Paul had and that he urged others to share are joy and peace in Christ Jesus.

Philippians can also help us to understand the Church. The letter (or letters) is largely concerned with the ongoing relationship between Paul the apostle and a community that he had founded. We see various facets of Paul's personality—ambivalent about receiving a gift, loving toward his friends in Christ, fearless in the face of death, annoyed and frustrated with some other Christians, and angry at what he regarded as a fundamental misunderstanding of Jesus and the gospel.

We also see the kinds of problems that early Christians faced: confusion about the heart of the gospel, internal dissensions and factions, and the challenge of fostering unity of hearts and minds. We glimpse the system of communication that the early Christians developed to allow the work of evangelism to continue and progress. And we have the earliest New Testament reference to "bishops and deacons" (1:1).

Prayer: God the Father of our Lord Jesus Christ, we praise and thank you for the gift of Christ Jesus, your Son and Servant. By becoming one of us—even to the point of dying on the cross for us, he opened up a new way of relating to you and to one another. By sharing his life and by being formed by that life and example, we know how to respect and serve one another. Christ Jesus is the source of our deepest joy and peace.

Free us from confusion and dissension. Help us to focus on Christ Jesus. Let him form us so that we may face our fears and even death itself with full confidence in your love for us. We make these prayers through Christ our Lord. Amen.

III

The Letter to the Colossians

Colossae was a city in western Asia Minor (modern Turkey), about 110 miles east of Ephesus. It was located in the upper Lycus River Valley, ten miles east of Laodicea and twelve miles southeast of Hierapolis. In the fifth century B.C. and later Colossae was regarded as an important city. But it was gradually outstripped by Laodicea and Hierapolis, and by the first century A.D. was considered a smaller town. A severe earthquake in A.D. 60 or 61 may have contributed further to its decline.

The Christian community at Colossae was apparently founded by Paul's co-worker Epaphras (see 1:7-8). From the lack of references to the Old Testament in the letter it seems that the Christians there were Gentile in background. Nevertheless, according to the Roman writer Cicero (*Pro Flacco* 68), there was a large Jewish population in the area. The letter to the Colossians, which was meant to be circulated in the neighboring cities (see 4:16), is best read in my opinion as a warning to Gentile Christians against the attractions of an esoteric Judaism that may have had elements taken from pagan philosophy and Greek mystery religions (see the exposition of 2:6-23).

The letter to the Colossians is attributed to Paul and Timothy (1:1), though most of it is written in the first person singular ("I"). If it was written directly by Paul, it

must have been composed during one of his imprisonments for the sake of the gospel ("I am in prison," 4:3)—
perhaps at Caesarea or Rome, or more likely at Ephesus
where he wrote to Philemon and to the Philippians in the
mid-50's of the first century.

And yet there are good reasons for supposing that the
letter was pseudonymous, that is, written under Paul's
name by an admirer or someone close to Paul. The practice
of imitating the style and thought of a famous author was
encouraged in the schools of antiquity. Except in the very
highest literary circles, the modern Western concepts of
intellectual property and individual authorship were foreign. To say what Paul would have said in a new situation
around A.D. 80 was a way of honoring his memory and
demonstrating the vitality of his thought.

The letter to the Colossians is very much in the spirit
of Paul. Indeed, it most likely originated in the Pauline
"school" based in Ephesus. It uses much from the language
and theology of Paul. And it addressed a real situation in
the Lycus Valley area. It provided sound theological and
pastoral advice to Gentile Christians there, who were
trying to discern their true identity with respect to the
intellectual and social attractions of an esoteric Judaism.

If Paul was not the author, we cannot be sure who was,
beyond the fact that he was close to Paul. The names of
Timothy (1:1) and Epaphras (1:7-8) have been suggested. Yet,
though the author admired and imitated Paul, he was not
content to repeat what Paul thought and wrote. In several
respects, while following Paul, he found his own distinctive
theological voice. Instead of the term "gospel," he preferred
"mystery," which he linked to the proclamation of Christ
among the Gentiles (see 1:27). He emphasized the universal

NEW CITY PRESS
202 CARDINAL RD.
HYDE PARK NY 12538

Thank you for choosing this book.
If you would like to receive regular information
about New City Press titles, please fill in this card.

Title purchased: _____

Please check the subjects
that are of particular interest to you:

- [ ] **FATHERS OF THE CHURCH**
- [ ] **CLASSICS IN SPIRITUALITY**
- [ ] **CONTEMPORARY SPIRITUALITY**
- [ ] **THEOLOGY**
- [ ] **SCRIPTURE AND COMMENTARIES**
- [ ] **FAMILY LIFE**
- [ ] **BIOGRAPHY / HISTORY**

Other subjects of interest: _____

(please print)

Name: _____

Address: _____

_____

_____

and cosmic (rather than the eschatological) significance of Christ (see 1:15-20), the present (rather than the future) dimension of salvation (see 2:11-13; 3:1), the Church as the world-wide body (rather than the local community as the body of Christ) with Christ as its head (see 1:18, 24; 2:19; 3:15), and Christian baptism (see 3:9-17) and "good order" (see 3:18–4:1) as important reasons for Christian action (rather than reward at the last judgment). If not composed by Paul himself, the letter is the earliest example of the reception and adaptation of Paul's theology in the early Church. Of course, the question of authorship in no way detracts from the work's status as Christian Scripture.

The letter to the Colossians follows the usual outline of Paul's letters. After the greeting (1:1-2), there is a thanksgiving (1:3-8) and petition (1:9-11). The first part of the body of the letter (1:12–2:23) deals with "doctrinal" matters. It begins with the quotation of an early Christian hymn about Christ as the Wisdom of God (1:15-20), surrounded by two applications of it (1:12-14; 1:21-23). Then it presents two reflections on Paul as a minister of the gospel (1:24-29; 2:1-5). The climax of the first part is the polemical refutation of the false "philosophy" and the positive presentation of Christian life as participation in Christ's death and resurrection (2:6-23). The second part of the body (3:1—4:1) concerns "ethical" matters. After a theological foundation (3:1-4), there are lists of vices to be avoided (3:5-11) and virtues to be pursued (3:12-17), along with a "household code" (3:18–4:1). The letter ends with concluding exhortations (4:2-6) along with travel plans and related messages (4:7-18).

In the exposition that follows I refer to the writer sometimes as "Paul" and sometimes as "the author." This practice reflects the dispute about authorship as well as the fact that the writer felt that he was saying what Paul would have said in the situation.

Greeting (1:1-2)

> [1] Paul, an apostle of Christ Jesus by the will of God, and Timothy our brother, [2] to the holy ones and faithful brothers in Christ in Colossae: grace to you and peace from God our Father.

The greeting follows the outline that is customary in the Pauline letters: the senders (1:1), the recipients (1:2a), and the greeting proper (1:2b). The greeting in Colossians is short and straightforward, without the embellishments found in other letters (see Rom 1:1-7; 1 Cor 1:1-3; Phil 1:1-2; Gal 1:1-5).

The greeting starts by invoking the apostolic authority of Paul: "an apostle of Christ Jesus by the will of God." Whereas in Philemon Paul is a "prisoner" and in Philippians he is a "servant," here he is an "apostle." In contrast to other letters where Paul's apostleship had been contested (Galatians, Romans, 1 and 2 Corinthians), here there is no indication that Paul's apostleship is a matter of controversy. The letter puts forward Paul the minister of the gospel as a figure of great moral authority. As in other letters (2 Corinthians, Philippians, 1 and 2 Thessalonians, Philemon) Timothy appears as a co-author. But the body of the letter is mainly in the first-person ("I"), and even the "we" references in the text do not prove joint authorship or a large role for Timothy in the letter's composition. The mention of Timothy, however, does establish the public nature of the letter. It comes not only from Paul but also from Timothy, another member of the apostolic team. The letter is to be read publicly at Colossae and Laodicea (4:16).

The addressees are "the holy ones and faithful brothers in Christ in Colossae." The word "saints" or "holy ones" is a customary way of referring to Christians, and "faithful brothers (and sisters)" is a parallel expression. The combination expresses God's role in making Christians "holy," and the kind of response (fidelity) demanded by the holiness of God. The qualifying expression "in Christ" is really the subject of the entire letter. The letter shows that through and in their common faith life has changed for the Colossians—the way in which they look at the world and how they behave. Their holiness and fidelity are linked to the death and resurrection of Christ. What joins them together as brothers and sisters is their faith and the ways of acting that it entails.

The greeting proper combines the key words from the conventions of Greek letters ("grace") and Hebrew letters ("peace"). In their Christian context they take on a theological significance: God's act of favor toward humankind ("grace") in Christ Jesus makes possible the "peace" that flows from right relationship with God.

Thanksgiving (1:3-8)

> [3]We always give thanks to God, the Father of our Lord Jesus Christ, when we pray for you, [4]for we have heard of your faith in Christ Jesus and the love that you have for all the holy ones [5]because of the hope reserved for you in heaven. Of this you have already heard through the word of truth, the gospel, [6]that has come to you. Just as in the whole world it is bearing fruit and

growing, so also among you, from the day you heard it and came to know the grace of God in truth, [7] as you learned it from Epaphras, our beloved fellow slave, who is a trustworthy minister of Christ on your behalf and [8] who also told us of your love in the Spirit.

For information about thanksgivings and petitions in the beginning of letters in antiquity and about Christian adaptations of this convention, see the discussion of Philemon 4–7. Whereas in Philemon the thanksgiving is a single verse (4) and is accompanied immediately by a petition (5-7), in Colossians much more space is given to the thanksgiving (1:3-8) and the petition (1:9-11).

The thanksgiving in Colossians 1:3-8 is one long and somewhat awkward sentence. The main verb is the very first word ("we give thanks"). It is accompanied by participles ("praying" and "having heard") to which the rest of the sentence is attached. The first part of the thanksgiving (1:4-5a) refers to the triad of Christian virtues—faith, love, and hope. The second part (1:5b-8) concerns the spreading of the gospel. There are references to God the Father (1:3), Christ Jesus (1:3, 4, 7), and the Holy Spirit (1:8).

The thanksgiving is cast in the first person plural form ("we"), which in Paul's letters is somewhat unusual (but see 1 Thes 1:2; 2 Thes 1:3). Every time ("always") Paul prays for the Colossians, he thanks God for them. The combination of "faith" and "love" appears in Philemon 5 (see also 2 Thes 1:3). Here the objects of faith ("in Christ Jesus") and love ("all the holy ones") are clear. For the triad of faith, love, and hope, see 1 Thessalonians 1:3; 5:8; and 1 Corinthians 13:13. This was obviously a traditional combination in early Christianity. In 1:5 "hope" refers to the fullness of life in God's kingdom (see also 3:1-4). Here the emphasis is more spatial ("in heaven") than temporal (the future Day of the Lord).

This teaching is said to be part of the gospel that the Colossians heard from Epaphras before they heard the false gospel now being preached among them. Indeed the purpose of the letter is to establish the "word of truth, the gospel" (1:5) over against the errors being taught at Colossae. The thanksgiving goes on to establish the apostolic tradition from Paul through Epaphras (1:7) and identifies that gospel as the same one that is bearing fruit and increasing throughout the world. In 1:6 it is called "the grace of God in truth." The idea of the gospel as "bearing fruit and growing" (see Mk 4:8; Acts 6:7; 12:24; 19:20) is that the progress of the gospel occurring all over the world prepares for the emphasis on the cosmic Christ outlined in 1:15-20 and developed as the letter proceeds.

The name Epaphras (1:7) is a shortened form of Epaphroditus. He is mentioned in 4:12 as "one of you" (from Colossae?) and in Philemon 23 as a "fellow prisoner" (confined with Paul, or merely in the same place?). He may be the same as the Epaphroditus mentioned in Philippians 2:25-30. In Colossians he is called a "fellow slave" and a faithful minister of the gospel. He seems to have brought the gospel to Colossae. Epaphras was apparently the one who had informed Paul about their love toward "all the holy ones" (1:4).

Besides observing convention and expressing a personal greeting, the thanksgiving in Colossians (as in the other Pauline letters) serves thematic and relational functions. The major issue in the body of the letter is the truth of the gospel. The contention of the letter writer is that the gospel that the Colossians heard first from Epaphras (the Pauline gospel) is the true gospel. The alternative teaching being presented at Colossae is false, despite its claims to universal significance. In fact, according to the letter to the Colossians, the world-wide gospel is the one that the Colossians heard from Epaphras.

A secondary theme is the kind of behavior that is consistent with that gospel. By praising the Colossians for their faith, love and hope (1:4-5), Paul indicates that the true gospel has already manifested itself in the Colossians' behavior. By singling out their "love in the Spirit" (1:8) that he learned from Epaphras' report, Paul reinforces the idea that faith in the gospel shows itself in loving deeds toward others.

The thanksgiving also supplies information about the relationships among the principal characters. Paul the apostle (1:1) and prisoner (4:10, 18) writes to the Colossian Christians, who apparently had received the gospel not from Paul directly but through his co-worker Epaphras. Epaphras is now with Paul and has given Paul a report about the achievements and problems of the Colossian community.

The situation and themes included in 1:3-8 provide rich themes for actualization: the practice of thanking God for and praying on behalf of other Christians, the importance of faith and hope in Christian life, the cosmic and dynamic nature of the gospel, and hope as the horizon of Christian existence.

Petition (1:9-11)

⁹Therefore from the day we heard this, we do not cease praying for you and asking that you may be filled

with the knowledge of his will through all spiritual wisdom and understanding [10]to live in a manner worthy of the Lord, so as to be fully pleasing, in every good work bearing fruit and growing in the knowledge of God, [11]strengthened with every power, in accord with his glorious might for all endurance and patience, with joy.

The petition proper (1:9-11) accompanies the thanksgiving (1:3-8), and the two may be seen as one unit (as in Phlm 4-7). Since what follows in 1:12-23 is joined to 1:11 by a participial construction ("giving thanks" in 1:12), it is possible to take the whole of 1:3-23 as the thanksgiving-petition.

The petition proper is one long sentence. It begins with the main verb ("we do not cease") plus two participles ("praying" and "asking") and a purpose clause ("that you may be filled") that gives the content of the petition ("the knowledge of his will"). The content is then spelled out by an infinitival clause ("to live in manner worthy of the Lord") along with two participial clauses ("bearing fruit and growing" and "strengthened").

The language of the petition echoes that of the thanksgiving. The most obvious example is the use of "bearing fruit and growing" in 1:10 with respect to Christian life—the same terms used in 1:6 to describe the progress of the gospel in all the world and in Colossae in particular. Other verbal links include "all" (1:4, 6; 1:9, 10, 11), "from the day" (1:6; 1:9), "hear" (1:4, 6; 1:9), "knowledge" (1:6; 1:9), and "praying " (1:3; 1:9).

The petition begins in 1:9 with the same verb that was used in 1:3 ("praying"). The prayer arises from what Paul has heard about the Colossians (see 1:4, 8) and is thus offered as an example of the apostle's prayer on their behalf (see 1:3). For those whom he addresses, the imprisoned apostle wishes "knowledge" (1:9; see Phlm 1:6; Phil 1:9; Eph 1:17). The hope that they will be "filled" with this knowledge anticipates the theme of "fullness" mentioned in 1:19 and developed in 2:9-10.

In 1:10 the biblical idiom for good conduct ("walk worthily"), when placed beside the three terms for knowledge in 1:9 ("knowledge ... spiritual wisdom ... understanding"), emphasizes the close relation between what one knows and what one does. The "Lord" here is most likely Christ, though in another context it could be taken as referring to God. The expression "fully pleasing" in 1:10 suggests that right conduct arising from right knowledge is pleasing to God. The goal of good deeds is to please God. The words "bearing fruit and growing" used in 1:6 with regard to the gospel are now used with regard to the Christians at Colossae.

The three related words in 1:11 "strengthened," "power," and "might" suggest that the origin of strength is God, and the goal of the strengthening is God's glory. Some interpreters discern a difference between "endurance" (toward external threats) and "patience" (toward problems within the community).

One of the literary functions of the petition is to prepare for major themes developed in the body of the letter. In doing so, the petition in 1:9-11 outlines a theology of Christian life. True knowledge, wisdom, and understanding have as their object the will of God, not the secrets of the universe or esoteric doctrines. True knowledge leads to behavior that pleases God, not oneself. It is fruitful and grows. The source of this knowledge and the power by which it is put into practice is God, who makes patient endurance possible. The allusion to fullness in 1:9 ("that you may be filled") gives the petition a christological dimension, since according to 1:19 all the fullness of God was pleased to dwell in Christ and according to 2:9-10 Christians have come to fullness of life in Christ. The emphasis on "full knowledge" prepares for what is in dispute at Colossae: Is the truth to be found in the Pauline gospel proclaimed by Epaphras or in the new teaching of the opponents?

Effects of the Christ-Event I (1:12-14)

12 ... giving thanks to the Father, who has made you fit to share in the inheritance of the holy ones in light. 13 He delivered us from the power of darkness and transferred us to the kingdom of his beloved Son, 14 in whom we have redemption, the forgiveness of sins.

The second "thanksgiving" (1:12-14) introduces the hymn (1:15-20) that serves as the main text for the letter body. The hymn focuses on Christ and the effects of his activity in creation and redemption; it is flanked by reflections (1:12-14; 1:21-23) on what the Christ-event means in the lives of Christians.

The first reflection (1:12-14) is introduced by a participial phrase ("giving thanks") that by syntax belongs with the participles of 1:10-11 or even 1:3 ("praying"). Thus it continues the long sentence that started in 1:9 (or the unit that began in 1:3). Despite the syntax, a new thought-unit begins in 1:12. Its use of "giving thanks" carries the notion of confession or proclamation of God's mighty acts (see Mt 11:25). In the New Testament (except in the Johannine writings) it is unusual to refer to God as "the Father" without qualification. The initiative in the process of redemption is God's ("who made you fit to share"). Since those addressed were predominantly Gentile Christians, the expression traces the Gentile mission to the action of God. The terms "inheritance" (understood spiritually) and "holy ones" are common in the Dead Sea scrolls. The "holy ones" dwell in the "light" as opposed to the "darkness" (1:13). There is probably a baptismal reference here.

The idea behind both "power" and "kingdom" in 1:13 is the sphere of influence, the spiritual side or camp in which one dwells. Here Christ as "his beloved Son" functions as the equivalent of the "Prince of Light" mentioned in Jewish texts.

In 1:14 the term "redemption" relates to the purchase of someone out of slavery ("ransom"). Used in a theological context (as in Rom 3:24; 8:23; 1 Cor 6:20; 7:23), it refers to what God has done in the Christ-event: Those who were in spiritual slavery have been set free. Behind the image may be the Old Testament idea of the "redeemer" (*go'el*), the relative who had the duty to buy back kin who had fallen into slavery. The "forgiveness of sins" further defines the bondage (sin) from which Christ redeems us (see also Rom 3:25; Eph 1:7). The forgiveness of sins is associated with John's baptism in Mark 1:4 and with baptism in Jesus' name in Acts 2:38.

The religious assumptions and terminology underlying 1:12-14 are paralleled by the "Instruction on the Two Spirits," found in the *Community Rule* 3–4 among the Dead Sea scrolls from Qumran. The idea is that God, the creator and sovereign Lord, has placed humankind under the rule of two spirits: "The origin of truth is in a fountain of light, and the origin of perversity is from a fountain of darkness." The children of righteousness are under the dominion of the Prince of Light and walk in the ways of light and do the deeds of light, whereas the children of perversity are under the power of the Angel of Darkness and walk in the ways of darkness and do the deeds of darkness. Belonging to either of these dominions is described frequently as sharing in their "inheritance" or "lot": "into their divisions all their hosts are divided.... God has allotted these (two spirits) in equal parts until the final end."

There are important Christian adaptations of this schema in 1:12-14. First, Christ Jesus as God's beloved Son fulfills the role assigned to the Prince of Light as the leader or captain of the children of light. Second, if we assume that most of those addressed in the letter to the Colossians were Gentiles, then the scope of those who may share in the lot of the saints has been expanded considerably beyond the sect of righteous Essenes in Palestine. Third, the dominion of darkness is sin, and the dominion of light is life in Christ (which involves redemption and forgiveness of sins). Finally, the dominion of light can be enjoyed in the present time, not only in the future, by those who through Christ belong to the lot of the saints in the light.

The most obvious theological teaching in 1:12-14 concerns the effects of the Christ-event (Jesus' death and resurrection). It has enabled Gentiles to find forgiveness of sins and thus become members in the dominion of God's beloved Son. The darkness and light imagery, the transfer from one dominion to another, and the idea of forgiveness of sins all suggest a connection with baptism. Whereas these Gentiles were slaves of sin, now through

Christ they have been forgiven their sins and freed from the power of darkness. At least this kind of theological language is made concrete in baptism. The baptismal flavor of this text also suggests that the hymn in 1:15-20 may have been used in connection with baptismal rituals.

The Christ Hymn (1:15-20)

[15]He is the image of the invisible God, the firstborn of all creation. [16]For in him were created all things in heaven and on earth, the visible and the invisible, whether thrones or dominions or principalities or powers; all things were created through him and for him. [17]He is before all things, and in him all things hold together. [18]He is the head of the body, the church.

He is the beginning, the firstborn from the dead, that in all things he himself might be preeminent. [19]For in him all the fullness was pleased to dwell, [20]and through him to reconcile all things for him, making peace by the blood of his cross [through him], whether those on earth or those in heaven.

The two main parts of this text (originally a hymn; see below) concern the role of Christ in creation (1:15-18a) and in redemption (18b-20). Each part begins with a "He is" clause (1:15a, 18b) that features the word "firstborn"—"of all creation" (15a) and "from the dead" (18b). Then there are reasons ("for") in 1:16 and 1:19 and conclusions in 1:17a-18a and 1:20. The word "all" runs through the text, serving as the basis for later reflections on Christ's cosmic rule.

The hymn was probably introduced by a blessing to which the two main clauses were attached: "Blessed be Our Lord Jesus Christ...." The idea of personified Wisdom as the image of God appears in Wisdom 7:26 ("the image of his goodness"). There may be some influence from Genesis 1:26 and Platonic thought, though neither is as influential as the Jewish personification of Wisdom. The phrase "the firstborn of all creation" in 1:15 evokes what is said in Proverbs 8:22: "The Lord begot me, the firstborn of his ways." The same kind of language appears in Sirach 24, Wisdom 7, and 1 Enoch 42 (a large Jewish apocalypse). The emphasis is on the superiority of Wisdom over creation rather than on the creaturehood of Wisdom. The one who was first in creation (Christ) is also first in redemption (1:18b-20).

In "in him were created all things" (1:16) the introductory phrase "in him" is probably instrumental, the equivalent of "through him" later in the verse. This claim about Christ's role in creation arises from the identification of Jesus as Wisdom, the agent in God's creation ("I was beside him as his craftsman," Prv 8:30). The same claim appears in John 1:1-3 with regard to Jesus as the Word (= Wisdom) of God. What follows in 1:16 emphasizes that "in him were created all things"—the heavenly and earthly, the visible and invisible. The listing of the various angelic "super-powers" (thrones, dominions, principalities, powers) serves to assert the sovereignty of Christ over all creation. Not only was Christ the instrument of their creation ("through him") but he is also the goal of their creation ("for him").

According to 1:17 Christ was not only at the origin of creation ("before all things") but he also keeps creation together in the present ("in him all things hold together"). What is in the background here is the idea of Wisdom as a "world soul" holding the world together and animating it, as in Wisdom 7:24: "Wisdom is mobile beyond all motion; and she penetrates and pervades all things by reason of her purity."

Calling Christ the "head of the body" (1:18a) assumes that the world is a body directed by Wisdom. The "head" gives direction to the whole cosmos. The identification of the body as the Church is a distinctively Christian interpretation of the image and gives the Church a cosmic dimension beyond its existence in local communities.

The order of redemption (1:18b-20) has been set in motion by the resurrected Christ ("the firstborn from the dead"). His resurrection as the "first fruits" (see 1 Cor 15:20, 23) initiates the order of reconciliation and stands as the pledge for the general resurrection. The description of the risen Christ as "preeminent" means that just as in the order of creation Christ as the Wisdom of God was first, so in the order of redemption the risen Christ is first.

In second-century gnosticism the "fullness" refers to the heavenly region between God and the world. But here there is no geographical sense. The idea is that the fullness of God (see 2:9) dwells in Christ: What God is, is present in Christ (see Jn 1:1).

The verb "reconcile" in 1:20 refers to a change in relationships. Though generally used in the social or political spheres, here it appears in a cosmic context (see Rom 5:10-11; 11:15; 2 Cor 5:18-19). The effect of the expression "by the blood of his cross" is to specify Jesus' death as the means by which the cosmic reconciliation has taken place. The background is Leviticus 17:11: "It is the blood, as the seat of life, that makes atonement." This theme is taken up in Hebrews 9:22: "Without the shedding of blood there is no forgiveness." The same point is made in

Romans 3:25: "... whom God set forth as an expiation, through faith, by his blood, to prove his righteousness because of the forgiveness of sins previously committed."

There is a consensus among scholars that 1:15-20 contains an early Christian hymn about Christ's role in creation and redemption. This conclusion is based on the unusual vocabulary, the parallel structures, the introductory relative clauses in Greek ("who is" in 1:15a, 18b) and the rhythmic quality of the language. There is also a consensus that the hymn has been slightly modified in the process of being incorporated into the letter. The identification of the "body" in 1:18 as the Church and the reference to "the blood of his cross" in 1:20 help to tie the hymn more directly to Christian life and to the Christ-event. The original hymn may have been used in the setting of baptismal ceremonies; this association is at least suggested by the introduction in 1:12-14. In the letter as it now stands, the hymn stands as the "text" to be explicated and developed in the rest of the letter.

The first part of the text (1:15-18a) applies to Christ Jesus what is said about personified Wisdom in Proverbs 8:22-31; Sirach 24; Wisdom 7; and 1 Enoch 42:1-3. This same Wisdom Christology appears also in John 1:1-18 and Hebrews 1:1-4. In the Jewish texts Wisdom is a female figure—perhaps because in both Hebrew and Greek the words for "wisdom" are feminine in gender, possibly to combat the popularity of the cult of the goddess Isis. All the Jewish wisdom texts attribute to Wisdom a role at creation and a superiority over all creation. Some texts (especially Wisdom 7) assign to Wisdom an ongoing role in sustaining creation as a kind of world-soul. This point suggests that Greek philosophical ideas (especially the cosmos as a gigantic body directed by the Word or Logos) may have also been part of the background of the first part of the hymn.

Despite their common themes the Jewish wisdom texts do not present a uniform picture of where Wisdom is to be found and what Wisdom is. According to Sirach 24, Wisdom is in the Jerusalem Temple at Mount Zion (24:10-11) and is the Law commanded through Moses (24:23). In Wisdom 7, the figure of Wisdom is everywhere, permeating creation and functioning as a world-soul. According to 1 Enoch 42:1-3, the dwelling place of Wisdom is heaven, and Wisdom is the heavenly mysteries. The modified hymn in Colossians 1:15-20 identifies Christ as Wisdom and locates him in the Church (1:18). So the first part of the hymn represents the Christian contribution to the Jewish debate about the place and identity of Wisdom.

The second part (1:18b-20) is more distinctively Christian in that it takes its starting point from the resurrection of Christ. Resurrection, of course, is a Jewish idea. Though there are many variations, the basic point is that at the end of history as we know it, and with the full coming of God's kingdom, God will raise up the dead and render a final judgment upon them: eternal life for the righteous and eternal punishment or annihilation for the wicked (see Dn 12:1-3). That an individual should be resurrected before the end of human history and the coming of the kingdom in its fullnesss went beyond Jewish beliefs about resurrection. The Christian claim is that in the resurrection of Jesus God has anticipated or begun the process of bringing the fullness of the kingdom.

The first part of the hymn contains some rich theological themes: Christ as the Wisdom of God, his pre-existence and role in creation, and the body of Christ. The second part of the hymn claims that the one in whom all the fullness of God dwells (1:19) has through his resurrection from the dead brought about the reconciliation of the entire cosmos to God. By identifying the body of Christ as the Church (1:18a), the present text anchors the cosmic thinking of the original hymn in the place where the writer and the readers meet. By insisting on the "blood of his cross" (1:20) as the means of reconciliation, the present text asserts Paul's theology of the cross (see 1 Cor 1:18–2:5) and avoids any separation between Jesus' death and resurrection. Reflecting on the significance of these themes in Christian life is the principal task of the rest of the letter to the Colossians.

Effects of the Christ-Event II (1:21-23)

[21] And you who once were alienated and hostile in mind because of evil deeds [22] he has now reconciled in his fleshly body through his death, to present you holy, without blemish, and irreproachable before him, [23] provided that you persevere in the faith, firmly grounded, stable, and not shifting from the hope of the gospel that you heard, which has been preached to every creature under heaven, of which I, Paul am a minister.

The second reflection on the effects of the Christ-event (1:21-23) is the counterpart of 1:12-14, and between them is sandwiched the hymn quoted in 1:15-20. This reflection begins a series of developments and adaptations of terms and ideas mentioned in 1:15-20. The second reflection is one long sentence consisting of an introductory clause in 1:21 ("you who once were..."), the main verb ("he has now reconciled") and a purpose clause ("to present you") in 1:22, and a conditional clause ("provided that you persevere") in 1:23. The most important word is the main verb ("reconciled"), which serves to make personal and concrete the cosmic reconciliation celebrated in 1:20.

In 1:21 the term "alienated" refers to the addressees' former condition as Gentiles (see Eph 2:12; 4:18). They were not innocent objects of divine hostility. Rather, they were hostile to God in an active way through their attitude that expressed itself in evil deeds (see Rom 1:18-32).

The verb "reconciled" in 1:22 applies the process of cosmic reconciliation mentioned in 1:20 to the Pauline mission to the Gentiles. Through Christ, God has made a new relationship possible between God and the Gentiles. The words "holy" and "without blemish" in 1:22 are cultic terms and fit with the verb "present," which can carry the idea of presenting a sacrifice (see Rom 12:2). The third word ("irreproachable") evokes the context of a legal proceeding, and also fits with "present"—especially in respect to the final judgment (see 1 Cor 8:8; 2 Cor 4:14; Rom 14:10).

The condition laid down in 1:23 is that believers remain firm in faith and hope (see 1:4-5). The term "firmly grounded" conveys that idea of the foundation of a building (see 1 Cor 3:10-15; Eph 2:20). The "faith" is the apostolic faith preached to them as the gospel by Epaphras. The "hope" is the fullness of God's kingdom promised in that gospel (see 1:5; 3:1-4). To say that the gospel had been preached to "every creature under heaven" is an exaggeration, since the Pauline mission reached only part of the Mediterranean world. But here (see 1:6; also Mk 16:15) there is an echo of the cosmic language contained in 1:15-20. The designation of Paul as a "minister" of the gospel is unusual. Its effect is to tie the process described in 1:12-23 to his ministry and to prepare for the following reflections on Paul's ministry in 1:24–2:5.

The hymn in 1:15-20 never tells us what needed reconciliation or why it was necessary. The second reflection focuses on the need for non-Jews or Gentiles to be reconciled to God, for they were "alienated and hostile in mind because of evil deeds." The term "body" so prominent in 1:18 appears in this reflection and is tied to the death of Christ on the cross ("in his fleshly body through his death"). The earthly aspect of the cosmic reconciliation effected by Christ (see 1:16, 20) is related to the gospel and to the Pauline mission.

The second reflection is an example of the "once/then" and "now" pattern found frequently in Paul's letters (Rom 6:17-22; 7:5-6; 11:30; Gal 4:8-9). The pattern appears again in 2:13 and is developed even further in Ephesians 2:1-22. Its occurrences in 1 Peter 1:14-25 and 2:10 indicate that the pattern was known and used outside the Pauline circle. The pattern appears also in the popular hymn "Amazing Grace," though there in an individualistic context foreign to the collective or communal setting of the New Testament cases.

In 1:21-23 the "once/then" and "now" pattern is applied to the Gentiles. It takes a very negative view of their past lives before receiving the gospel and accuses them of ignorance and wicked behavior. See Romans 1:18-32 for Paul's extended meditation on pagan life apart from the gospel. The basic claim is that through Christ's death God has reconciled the Gentiles to himself. Their reconciliation to God through Christ is part of the process of cosmic reconciliation brought about in Christ's resurrection from the dead and is thus a pledge toward the fullness of reconciliation that will accompany the last judgment.

Paul's Ministry I (1:24-29)

[24] Now I rejoice in my sufferings for your sake, and in my flesh I am filling up what is lacking in the afflictions of Christ on behalf of his body, which is the Church, [25] of which I am a minister in accordance with God's stewardship given to me to bring to completion for you the word of God, [26] the mystery hidden from ages and from generations past. But now it has been manifested to his holy ones, [27] to whom God chose to make known the riches of the glory of this mystery among the Gentiles; it is Christ among you, the hope for glory. [28] It is he whom we proclaim, admonishing everyone and teaching everyone with all wisdom, that we may present everyone perfect in Christ. [29] For this I labor and struggle, in accord with the exercise of his power working within me.

The first part of the "doctrinal" section of the letter features a hymn about Christ and two reflections on his effects in the lives of Christians (1:21-23). The third part (2:6-23) warns the Colossians against an erroneous and potentially dangerous teaching. In between (1:24–2:5) there is a reflection on Paul's ministry as an apostle, probably intended to establish the authority of Paul's gospel over against the false teaching being proposed at Colossae. In this second section Paul reflects first on his ministry to the Gentiles as proclaimer of Christ (1:24-29) and then somewhat more concretely on his relationship to the Colossian Christians (2:1-5).

The first reflection (1:24-29) begins with comments on Paul's suffering (1:24) and ends with comments on his hard work as apostle to the Gentiles (1:29). The center of the text (1:26-27) defines the mystery that has been revealed: "Christ in you" (Gentiles). The intervening verses (1:25, 28) define the origin, task, and goal of Paul's apostolic ministry. The apostle is in the service of the gospel.

After a somewhat abrupt beginning ("Now I rejoice") in 1:24, the text refers to "filling up what is lacking in the afflictions of Christ." The word "fill up" means to remedy a deficiency (see 1 Cor 16:17; 2 Cor 9:12; 11:9; Phil 2:30). The word "afflictions" is not used in the New Testament with reference to Jesus' passion and death. Rather, it is associated with the trying times that will precede the second coming of the Messiah (see Mk 13:8, 18-20, 24). The idea of the "woes" or trials connected with the Messiah's coming is found also in Jewish texts (see below). The identification of Christ's body as the Church was made in 1:18. Here the parallel expressions "for your sake" and "on behalf of his body, which is the Church" capture both the local and the universal dimensions of the Church.

In 1:25 the terms "minister" and "stewardship" with respect to Paul's activity are unusual, though the ideas are familiar. Paul generally speaks of himself as an "apostle" or "servant," not as a "minister" (but see 1:23). He generally speaks of the "grace" of apostleship that had been given to him, not the stewardship (but see 1 Cor 9:17). The word "completion" plays on "filling up" in 1:24. It also alludes to Paul's commission to preach the gospel of Jesus Christ "fully," that is, everywhere it had not been preached (see Rom 15:19). The gospel that Paul is to make fully known is given a definition in 1:26-27.

The "mystery that was long hidden but now revealed" according to 1:26-27 is "Christ in you," that is, the gospel made available in or among the Gentiles. Here the "holy ones" are those Gentiles who have received the gospel; Christ is now among such persons. The definition of the mystery is surrounded by exalted language ("the riches of the glory") and is further qualified as the pledge of future glory ("the hope for glory"). Thus in this context Christ is present in the gospel preached among the Gentiles.

Only in 1:28 of this section does the apostle speak in the plural, presumably to include those who had preached the gospel in Colossae (1:7) and Timothy (1:1). The threefold repetition of "everyone" is clearly emphatic and made more so by "with all wisdom." The goal of preaching Christ to the Gentiles was to open up for all persons the possibility of right relationship with God (justification). Paul wants to present every person as "perfect in Christ"— perfect in a distinctively Christian way.

The activist terms in the beginning of 1:29 ("I labor and struggle") are balanced by the recognition that God ("his power working within me") empowers the apostle in carrying out his task of proclaiming the gospel among the Gentiles. There may be a reference in the first part to Paul's practice of supporting himself by manual labor (see 1 Thes 2:9; 1 Cor 4:12; etc.).

The text raises two important questions: How can Paul fill up what is lacking in the Messiah's tribulations? Why does Paul refer to the preaching of the gospel to the Gentiles as a "mystery"?

100

Paul frequently quotes early Christian formulas to the effect that Christ died "for us" or "for our sins" (Rom 3:25-26; 1 Cor 11:24; 15:3; etc.). Paul himself uses similar expressions as part of his theological discourse (Rom 5:6; 14:15; 2 Cor 5:14, 21; Gal 1:4; 3:13; etc.). Paul also describes how he shared in the sufferings and resurrection of Jesus (2 Cor 1:5; Phil 3:10-11). But Colossians 1:24 seems to go beyond these claims to say that Paul suffers on behalf of the Colossian Christians and that he thus fills up what is lacking in Christ's tribulations.

In the light of what was said in 1:19-20 ("in him all the fullness was pleased to dwell, and through him to reconcile all things for him"), 1:24 cannot mean that there was something lacking about the reconciliation brought about by Christ.

The proper background for understanding 1:24 is the Jewish motif of the tribulations associated with the Messiah's coming. In Jewish texts the "woes" of the Messiah refer to the tribulations that must be endured before the Messiah comes (see *Mishnah Sotah* 9:10). In Mark 13 the idea is applied to the second coming of Christ (see Mk 13:8, 19-20, 24, and the parallels in Mt 24 and Lk 21). These tribulations have a fixed limit that is known to God alone. The time in which this quota may be fulfilled can be shortened by God "for the sake of the elect" (Mk 13:20).

In 1:24 Paul applies his sufferings and toils as an apostle to the quota of tribulations before the second coming of Christ, which will include the full vindication of Gentile Christians like the Colossians. Paul's sufferings are for the "good" of others. Rather than debating the sufficiency or insufficiency of Christ's sufferings, he is talking about how his sufferings as an apostle may be contributing to shortening the time before Christ's second coming.

The question why Paul refers to the preaching of the gospel to the Gentiles as a "mystery" can be clarified with reference to the book of Daniel. In Daniel 2 the word "mystery" is used several times (2:18, 19, 27-30, 47) to describe what God will do in the "last days" when the Seleucid empire comes to an end and dominion is handed over to the saints of the Most High (the righteous within Israel and perhaps also the heavenly hosts of angels).

Paul and other early Christians regarded Jesus' resurrection as the inauguration or anticipation of the fullness of God's kingdom, and viewed themselves as living in the "last days." God had revealed to Paul that Christ Jesus was to be proclaimed to Gentiles as well as Jews, and that Gentiles could thus become part of God's people. A divine mystery is not something that human beings figure out on their own. God must reveal it to them. In calling Paul to be the apostle to the Gentiles (1:25), God revealed the mystery about the gospel and its relevance for non-Jews: "Christ among you, the hope for glory" (1:27).

The first reflection on Paul's ministry (1:24-29) is an eloquent statement about his apostleship: total dedication to preaching the gospel to the Gentiles, lively involvement with the gospel and those who received it, the goal of presenting everyone "perfect" in Christ before God at the last judgment, and recognition of God's work in calling him and empowering him.

Paul's Ministry II (2:1-5)

> [1] For I want you to know how great a struggle I am having for you and for those in Laodicea and all who have not seen me face to face, [2] that their hearts may be encouraged as they are brought together in love, to have

all the richness of fully assured understanding, for the knowledge of the mystery of God, Christ, [3] in whom are hidden all the treasures of wisdom and knowledge. [4] I say this so that no one may deceive you by specious arguments. [5] For even if I am absent in the flesh, yet I am with you in spirit, rejoicing as I observe your good order and the firmness of your faith in Christ.

Whereas 1:24-29 focused on Paul's ministry in proclaiming Christ among the Gentiles, 2:1-5 concerns his relationship with the churches in the Lycus Valley (Colossae, Laodicea, etc.). Paul had not founded these churches, nor had he ever visited them in person. It was Epaphras who evangelized them (see 1:7).

In 2:1-5 it is possible to discern the kind of structure found also in 1:24-29. In 2:1 Paul mentions his toil on behalf of these churches, and in 2:5 he reminds them of his presence among them "in spirit." In 2:2 he claims that the goal of his toil was the Colossians' full knowledge of Christ as the mystery of God, and in 2:4 he warns against those who try to lead them astray from this knowledge. In the center (2:3) is the assertion that in Christ lay hidden (but will be revealed) all the treasures of wisdom and knowledge. As in 1:24-29, the center is Christ the Wisdom of God, in whose service the apostle labors.

The formula "I want you to know" in 2:1 appears also in 1 Corinthians 11:3 as an introduction to Paul's setting straight the community about a tradition. The noun "struggle" picks up the verb in 1:29. It is hard to know whether readers got the athletic metaphor (see 1 Tm 6:12; 2 Tm 4:7; Heb 12:1) or simply took it generically as "struggle." Although the letter is addressed to the Colossians (1:2), it was also intended for the neighboring city

103

of Laodicea (see 4:15-16). The problem combatted in the next section apparently faced Christians in the whole Lycus Valley region. These people as yet had no personal contact with Paul, and so belonged to the category of those "who have not seen me face to face."

The term "brought together" in 2:2 is used with reference to the body in 2:19 and Ephesians 4:16 in a strong metaphorical sense ("knit together"). The rest of the verse is deliberately overloaded to emphasize the themes of knowledge ("fully assured understanding ... knowledge of the mystery") and wealth ("all the richness"). The same themes appear in 2:3: "all the treasures of wisdom and knowledge" (see Rom 11:33). For the identity of Christ as the mystery of God, see 1:27: "Christ among you, the hope for glory." The hidden treasures in Christ (see Is 45:3; Sir 1:25) will be manifest on the Day of the Lord.

The warning in 2:4 against being deceived by specious arguments prepares for the attack in 2:6-23 (see Jas 1:22; 1 Cor 2:4). The expression in 2:5 about being absent in the flesh but present "in spirit" recalls 1 Corinthians 5:3. If "spirit" carries an allusion to the Holy Spirit, then the verse suggests that through the Holy Spirit the apostle and the readers are "brought together in love" (2:2). The words "good order" and "firmness" are sometimes used in military contexts. But the military image is not developed here (see Eph 6:10-17).

Christ the Wisdom of God binds together Paul the apostle and the Christians of Colossae, Laodicea, and other cities in the Lycus Valley. As noted earlier, Colossae was in southwest Asia Minor (modern Turkey), about 110 miles east of Ephesus. It was ten miles east of Laodicea (see 4:15-16) and twelve miles southeast of Hierapolis (see 4:13). According to ancient sources (Cicero's *Pro*

Flacco, 68), a large Jewish population lived in this area. This fact may have some bearing on the nature of teaching that is to be combatted.

The people addressed in this letter were new Christians and predominantly (if not entirely) Gentiles. The problem of the "false teaching" treated in 2:6-23 seems to apply to them. Paul had heard of their faith from others, especially from Epaphras (1:7), and so he felt an obligation to instruct them about what he regarded as perversion of the gospel. Whether 2:1-5 came directly from Paul or was composed by an admirer, it depicts the apostle spending himself on behalf of his fellow Christians and wishing them only the best. At the center of his consciousness is Christ the mystery of God, not himself. He is convinced that in Christ real wisdom is to be found and regards teachings that call this into question as dangerous delusions.

Warning I (2:6-15)

⁶So, as you received Christ Jesus the Lord, walk in him, ⁷rooted in him and built upon him and established in the faith as you were taught, abounding in thanksgiving. ⁸See to it that no one captivate you with an empty, seductive philosophy according to human tradition, according to the elemental powers of the world and not according to Christ.

⁹For in him dwells the whole fullness of the deity bodily, ¹⁰and you share in this fullness in him, who is the head of every principality and power. ¹¹In him you were also circumcised with a circumcision not administered by hand, by stripping off the carnal body, with the circumcision of Christ. ¹²You were buried with him in baptism, in which you were also raised with him through

faith in the power of God, who raised him from the dead. [13] And even when you were dead [in] transgressions and the uncircumcision of your flesh, he brought you to life along with him, having forgiven us all our transgressions; [14] obliterating the bond against us, with its legal claims, which was opposed to us, he also removed it from our midst, nailing it to the cross; [15] despoiling the principalities and the powers, he made a public spectacle of them, leading them away in triumph by it.

The warning against the false "philosophy" threatening the Colossian Christians can be divided into two parts (2:6-15; 2:16-23). We learn about the philosophy only indirectly, by means of the letter's refutation of it. The first part brings important elements of Pauline theology to bear on the matter.

The warning begins (2:6-7) by reminding the Colossians that the gospel that they received ("Christ Jesus is Lord") demands an appropriate response by way of action ("walk in him"). The warning proper (2:8) calls the "philosophy" a vain and empty delusion built on human tradition and the "elemental powers of the world." The reason why this philosophy can be ignored is that genuine "fullness" can be found only in Christ (2:9-10). The genuine circumcision is baptism into Christ's death and resurrection (2:11-12), which the Colossians have experienced as a coming to life out of death in sin (2:13a). The argument is sealed by an appeal to what may have been part of an early Christian hymn (2:13b-15) that explains what has happened to the Gentile Christians through the death of Christ.

In 2:6 the verb "received" refers to the tradition of faith that the Colossians were given (see 1 Cor 11:3; 15:1, 3;

Gal 1:9, 12; Phil 4:9; etc.). The content of the tradition is specified in the object of the verb: "Christ Jesus (is) the Lord." The word "walk" to describe appropriate conduct as a fitting response to God's grace is a common biblical metaphor. The four participles in 2:7 ("rooted ... built ... established ... abounding") describe the helps that the Colossian Christians have in their efforts at responding to God's grace and the gospel. For the combination of images of growth and building, see 1 Corinthians 3:6, 9.

As in Philippians 3:2, the verb "see to it" in 2:8 introduces a strong warning against the false teachers. Their action is described in graphic terms ("captivate" in the sense of "snare, trap, rob"). The term "philosophy" had a wide application in antiquity and could include religious teachings like Judaism and even early Christianity. The accompanying adjectives ("empty, seductive") gives the author's evaluation of the philosophy that was enticing the Colossians. The term "elemental powers" refers first to any series of things such as the letters of the alphabet. Then it came to be used for what were perceived as the basic building blocks of the universe: earth, air, water, and fire. In some circles the elements were personified into mythical and even demonic beings.

In 2:9 ("in him dwells the whole fullness of the deity bodily") the language of the hymn in 1:19 is now applied to Christ as the basis for the refutation of the rival philosophy. The specification "of the deity" clarifies 1:19: The fullness of God dwells in Christ; what God is, is present in Christ (see Jn 1:1). The adverb "bodily" is easy to translate but difficult to interpret. It could be taken as a simple adverb ("really"), an allusion to the Church as the body of Christ (see 1:18), or a reference to the incarnation (the physical body of Jesus). Since the fullness of God resides in Christ, only those who are in Christ can be filled. This is presented in 2:10 as a consequence of the doctrine of "fullness" in 1:19 and 2:9. The insistence on the "fullness" terminology suggests that it was part of the opponents' philosophy and therefore needed to be treated from the perspective of Christ. The description of Christ as the "head of every principality and power" in 2:10 combines phrases from 1:18 and 1:16. It asserts the sovereignty of Christ over all created beings.

The expression "not ... by hand" in 2:11 refers to divine rather than human action (see Dn 2:34, 45). Here it contrasts the physical/human/Jewish circumcision and the spiritual/divine/Christian baptism. Given the emphasis placed on the topic here, it is likely that circumcision was part of the opponents' "philosophy." Whereas physical circumcision strips away the tip of the male member, spiritual circumcision in Christ (baptism) removes that aspect of the human person ("the carnal body") that is opposed and hostile to God. Here only in the New Testament is baptism described as the "circumcision of Christ."

The teaching in 2:12 about identification with Christ's death and resurrection in baptism is a neat summary of Romans 6:1-11. The chief difference comes in the claim "you were also raised with him," which could suggest that the believer's resurrection has already taken place. In Romans 6:4 Paul avoids such an affirmation by focusing on appropriate activity in the present. The divine origin of the new life in Christ is made clear by the expression "through faith in the power of God." The Colossians' faith in the God who raised Jesus expressed itself in the baptism by which they shared in Christ's death and resurrection.

The description "dead in transgressions" and "uncircumcision" in 2:13 reflects Paul's evaluation of Gentile life apart from Christ (see 1 Thes 1:9; Rom 1:18-32). The language indicates that those who are in danger of being snared by the philosophy were Gentile Christians. The expression "he brought you to life along with him" has God as its subject and is a vivid climax to the main theme of 2:6-15. The participle "having forgiven us" introduces a series of participles (perhaps from an early Christian hymn) that celebrate what God has done in Christ. Forgiveness of sins leads the list and receives further explanation in what follows. The noun "transgressions" appears early in 2:13 and so links what was said about baptism and what follows in 2:13b-15.

The image of the "bond" in 2:14 is that of an I.O.U., binding upon and signed by the human race, and made out to God. This document contains legal stipulations that impose penalties upon the human race. Through Christ's death and resurrection, God has wiped this document away, thus clearing the slate and making possible a new relationship with God. The expression "nailing it to the cross" most likely alludes to the charge attached to the cross of Jesus: "the King of the Jews" (see Mk 15:26). From the perspective of Christian faith the bond was equivalent to the charge on which Jesus was killed. The interpretation of "it" as Jesus' body is less likely.

Whereas in 2:13b-14 the subject of the verbs is God, in 2:15 the subject is Christ. The New American Bible (revised) translation suggests a negative interpretation of the "principalities and powers." The idea is that by his death on the cross Christ despoiled those hostile forces and led them captive as a Roman general returning from battle led a parade not only of his armies but also of his captives and the spoils taken from them.

From this part of the warning we can infer some precepts of the "philosophy." It gave attention to the "elemental powers of the world" (2:8), talked about "fullness" (2:9), and practiced circumcision (2:11). The latter point suggests a connection with Judaism, and more Jewish elements appear in the second part of the warning.

The large Jewish community living in southwestern Asia Minor was attractive to non-Jews for various reasons: Judaism's reputation for wisdom and high ethical standards, the attractiveness of Jewish synagogue services, the festivities associated with the Sabbaths and holy days, and the esoteric knowledge (in matters of healing, magic, and astrology) ascribed to Jews.

The Gentiles most attracted to Pauline Christianity (which celebrated Jesus the Jew but did not require circumcision or full Torah observance) were probably gathered in large part from those who had been frequenting the synagogues previously (in Acts they are called "God fearers"). Such persons may have been interested in a "fuller" kind of Judaism after their conversion to Christianity. On the other hand, one can imagine other Gentiles who had first accepted the gospel and then learned about the Judaism from which it derived. Their desire to learn more about Judaism and to have more direct contacts with the synagogue may have alarmed the Christian teachers of the Pauline gospel. That Judaism was called a "philosophy" presents no obstacle, for so it was described by Philo and Josephus.

The Pauline response is "Christ alone!" Not only is Christ sufficient to bring Gentiles into right relationship with God but also renders any other way unneccesary. In him the fullness of divinity resides (2:9), and through him the Colossians have been filled (2:10). Thus the hymn cited in 1:15-20 is used to undergird the theological assertion of the text: Christ alone!

The passage restates some major points of Paul's theology: the connection between who one is in Christ and what one does (2:6-7) and the idea of sharing in Christ's death and resurrection through baptism (2:12-13). But there are also some new ideas: the notion of baptism as the better circumcision willed by God (2:11) and the concept that in baptism one is already raised (2:12). The text also gives extraordinary emphasis to Paul's theme of being "in Christ."

Warning II (2:16-23)

[16] Let no one, then, pass judgment on you in matters of food and drink or with regard to a festival or new moon or sabbath. [17] These are shadows of things to come; the reality belongs to Christ. [18] Let no one disqualify you, delighting in self-abasement and worship of angels, taking his stand on visions, inflated without reason by his fleshly mind, [19] and not holding closely to the head, from whom the whole body, supported and held together by its ligaments and bonds, achieves the growth that comes from God.

[20] If you died with Christ to the elemental powers of the world, why do you submit to regulations as if you were still living in the world? [21] "Do not handle! Do not taste! Do not touch!" [22] These are all things destined to perish with use; they accord with human precepts and teachings. [23] While they have semblance of wisdom in rigor of devotion and self-abasement [and] severity to

the body, they are of no value against gratification of the flesh.

The second part of the warning against the false "philosophy" (2:16-23) provides more indirect information about the problem and again appeals to identification with Christ in baptism (2:20) as its best refutation.

The first section (2:16-19) features two warnings: "Let no one pass judgment on you" (2:16) and "Let no one disqualify you" (2:18). The first warning characterizes the food laws and festivals as mere "shadows" in comparison with the "reality" that belongs to Christ. The second warning criticizes fasting and "worship of angels" as puffery because they ignore Christ the head from whom all divine growth comes.

The second section (2:20-23) appeals to baptism as death with Christ (2:20) and uses it as the basis for refusing to submit to human regulations about perishable things (2:20b-22) that lead only to indulgence of the flesh despite the claims made for them. The following section (3:1-4) appeals to baptism as resurrection with Christ.

The reference to "matters of food and drink" in 2:16 could be to Jewish ritual laws (pertaining to foods and vessels for drinking) or to ascetical practices undertaken in the hope of getting closer to God and receiving divine revelations. The two are not mutually exclusive, of course. In Romans 14:17 Paul says that "the kingdom of God is not a matter of food and drink but of righteousness, peace, and joy in the Holy Spirit." The list "festival or new moon or sabbath" suggests a clear connection with Judaism (see Hos 2:13; Ez 45:17; 1 Chr 23:31; 2 Chr 2:3; 31:3). For the idea of Old Testament figures and institutions as shadows of the realities to come in Christ (2:17), see Hebrews 8:5; 10:1.

The verb "disqualify" in 2:18 suggests the idea of disqualifying someone from an athletic contest. The term "self-abasement" (which in 3:12 is regarded as a virtue to be pursued) may here refer to the practice of fasting as part of the preparation for receiving visions from or about heaven, and so fits with what follows about "worship of angels." It is most unlikely that the angels were regarded as the objects of worship. Rather, the idea seems to be entering (in visions) the sphere where the angels worship God. By dismissing those who promote these practices as "inflated without reason" the text probably replies to their claims of "fullness." The accompanying phrase "by his fleshly mind" means that the "flesh" (the aspect of the person that is hostile to God and is thus the opposite of "spirit") rules over the minds of those who put their trust in such practices.

In 2:19 the text returns (see 2:10) to the affirmation made in the hymn (1:18) about Christ as the head of the body and develops the image of the body as organically attached to the head. It also introduces the idea of the head giving growth to the body—a growth in which God is the agent (for further development, see Eph 4:16).

For dying with Christ in baptism (2:20), see Romans 6:1-11. Observing the elemental regulations of the world places one still in the "world" understood as a negative sphere (where the "flesh" prevails). Baptism in Christ has taken the Christian out of this sphere of influence. The nature of the "regulations" are specified in the list in 2:21. The regulations are absolute statements, admitting no exceptions. The difference between "handle " and "touch" is difficult to discern.

The first part of 2:22 characterizes the objects of the prohibitions as transitory and ephemeral, since they get used up. The second part describes the origin of these precepts as human traditions (see Is 29:13; Mk 7:7; Mt 15:9). In 2:23 the practices are dismissed as self-made religion. Though they purport to give "fullness," in fact they only lead to indulgence and belong to the sphere of the "flesh."

The second part of the warning adds to the picture of the "philosophy" that is being opposed. It includes teachings about food and drink (2:16), observing certain Jewish festivals (2:16), fasting and visionary experiences (2:18), submitting to certain taboos (2:21), and other ascetical practices (2:23). These fit an esoteric Judaism with an emphasis on visions and participating in the heavenly worship.

The basic objection is that people who cultivate these practices are "not holding closely to the head" (2:19) and so are not part of the body (the Church) that God makes to grow. It is not so much the practices that are being condemned as it is the attitude of those who imagine that they can manipulate God apart from Christ. This is basic Pauline theology. Underlying the attack is the Pauline dualism between the "flesh" (opposed to God) and the "spirit" (responsive to God). Despite their claims of closeness to God, the opponents remain in the "flesh" because they do not hold fast to Christ the head of the body.

The warnings in 2:6-23 are polemical, written for a specific situation. They criticize an esoteric Judaism in western Asia Minor of the first century. They do not condemn all pious practices or asceticism, or all Judaism as such. They do criticize an attitude that seeks salvation apart from Christ the head and on the strength of human devices alone. The positive thrust of the text is identifying with Christ's death and resurrection in baptism and thus being opened to life in the Spirit.

Christian Life (3:1-4)

> [1] If then you were raised with Christ, seek what is above, where Christ is seated at the right hand of God. [2] Think of what is above, not of what is on earth. [3] For you have died, and your life is hidden with Christ in God. [4] When Christ your life appears, then you too will appear with him in glory.

The preceding warnings against the false philosophy appealed positively to Jesus' death and resurrection (2:13b-15) and to the believers' identification with them in baptism (2:11-13a, 20). Whereas the warnings seem to have been directed against a specific danger facing the Colossian community, the "ethical" teachings in the next part of the letter (3:1–4:1) are general and less bound to a particular situation. They provide advice about vices and virtues, and about the order of the household. Yet, at nearly every point they remind us how Christian behavior relates to Jesus' death and resurrection.

The theological basis for the teachings about Christian behavior is set forth in 3:1-4. Just as 2:20-23 began with a conditional clause ("if you died with Christ"), this section begins with a conditional clause ("if then you were raised with Christ"). In both 2:20-23 and 3:1-4 there is an allusion to baptism, and 3:1-4 draws a parallel between Christ and the believer on three counts: Christ has died, and you have died with him; Christ is risen, and you have been raised with him in baptism; and Christ will come again in glory, and you will share in his glorious coming. In the meantime—between the present and Christ's glorious second coming—the Christian life of resurrection and glory remains hidden "with Christ in God."

The assumption of 3:1 is that the addressees have been raised with Christ in baptism (see 2:12). Though this claim goes beyond what is said in Romans 6:1-11, the idea is still that the fullness of blessedness remains in the future. Some early Christians apparently even went further by saying (as in 2 Tm 2:18) that "the resurrection has already taken place." To seek "what is above" (3:1-2) is to set one's mind and heart on the things of the spirit/Spirit, and to orient one's life by them. The things "of earth" (3:2) belong to the realm of the "flesh." The idea that Christ is "seated at the right hand of God" alludes to Psalm 110:1—a text frequently used in the New Testament to describe the exaltation of the risen Christ (see Mt 22:44; Mk 12:36; Lk 20:42-43; Acts 2:34-35; 1 Cor 15:25; Heb 1:3, 13; 10:12).

The statement "you have died" in 3:3 refers to the idea of baptism as being buried with Christ (2:12, 20; see Rom 6:1-11). The risen life of the Christian remains hidden "with Christ in God," that is, not yet fully public. In the meantime Christians should set their minds and hearts on what is "above." The revelation of Christ expected in 3:4 is the second coming—the only reference to this in Colossians. At the second coming the fullness of the resurrected life enjoyed by Christians will be made manifest as part of the glory displayed by Christ, and they will share in and enjoy the glory of God. For glorification as the result of the Christ-event see Romans

8:30; for glory as part of the end-time vindication see Romans 8:18, 21 and 1 Thessalonians 2:12.

The spatial disjunction between "what is above" and "what is on earth" is unusual in Paul's letters (see also Jn 3:1-21). The more common Pauline disjunctions are "spirit" and "flesh," and "this world/age" and "the world/age to come." The spatial distinction here follows in part from the allusion to Psalm 110:1. Since the exalted Lord/Christ is at God's right hand, Christians must set their minds and hearts on him and "what is above" as part of their identification with the risen Christ. The second reading in the Church's lectionary for Easter Day is appropriately taken from 3:1-4.

Vices to Be Avoided (3:5-11)

> [5] Put to death, then, the parts of you that are earthly: immorality, impurity, passion, evil desire, and the greed that is idolatry. [6] Because of these the wrath of God is coming [upon the disobedient]. [7] By these you too once conducted yourselves, when you lived in that way. [8] But now you must put them all away: anger, fury, malice, slander, and obscene language out of your mouths. [9] Stop lying to one another, since you have taken off the old self with its practices [10] and have put on the new self, which is being renewed, for knowledge, in the image of its creator. [11] Here there is not Greek and Jew, circumcision and uncircumcision, barbarian, Scythian, slave, free; but Christ is all and in all.

Having laid the foundation for Christian ethics in Christ's death and resurrection (3:1-4), the author gives directions about the kinds of behavior that Christians should avoid. The most obvious structural principle is the series of three imperatives: "put to death" (3:5), "put away" (3:8), and "stop lying" (3:9). The first two imperatives introduce two lists of five vices to be avoided. In the sentence that begins with the third imperative, the real focus is on taking off the old self and putting on the new self. The implications of all this are drawn in 3:11 by what was probably a baptismal slogan (or something based on one).

The command to put to death "the parts of you that are earthly" in 3:5 flows from the nature of baptism as identification with Christ's death (see 3:3). Therefore whatever earthly tendencies remain (see 3:2) should be killed off. Of the five vices listed in 3:5, the first four concern immoral sexual activity. The fifth is greed, which is then linked to idolatry. Jews often described Gentile immorality in terms of sexual excess, greed, and idolatry. For other lists of vices see Galatians 5:19-21; 1 Corinthians 5:10-11; 2 Corinthians 12:21; Romans 1:29-31; and 1 Timothy 1:9-10. For some Jewish examples in the Dead Sea scrolls, see the *Community Rule* 4:9-11 and *Damascus Document* 4:17-18. Such vices are to be rooted out by Gentile Christians who have been raised with Christ in baptism and now seek "what is above."

As 3:6 indicates, one reason why these vices are to be rooted out is that practice of them leads to God's condemnation and punishment in the coming judgment (see Rom 2:5; 5:9; 1 Thes 1:10). But Paul understood God's wrath as already active and manifest in the world as punishment for sin (see Rom 1:18-32). In 3:7 the readers are reminded of their pagan past when they conducted themselves according to these vices. Now having been baptized, they no longer live that way. For the "once ... but now" pattern as applied to Christian conversion and baptism, see 1:21-23.

In 3:8 five more vices are condemned. It is possible to associate all five vices with speech, and so "out of your mouths" may relate to all five members of the list. Since these vices remained possibilities for Gentile Christians (and indeed all Christians), they needed to be warned against them.

Taking off the "old self" (3:9) refers in Romans 6:6 to what has been crucified with Christ and put aside in baptism. The image of "taking off" may allude to the change of garments at baptism. At any rate, the basic point is that baptism involves taking off one set of actions and putting on another set.

The fact that the "new self" (3:10) is being renewed and moving forward toward full knowledge is consistent with the perspective developed in 3:1-4. Since full knowledge is the goal, the ethical teachings presented here have significance for those making their way toward it. The idea of "in the image of its creator" is that God created a new humanity in and through Christ (see Gn 1:26). There is also a reference back to Christ as the image of the invisible God in 1:15.

The passage ends in 3:11 with an allusion to what must have been an early Christian baptismal formula. A similar formula appears in Galatians 3:28: "There is neither Jew nor Greek, there is neither slave nor free person, there is not male and female; for you are all one in Christ Jesus." The distinction in 3:11 between circumcision and uncircumcision is another way of saying "not Jew and Greek." The repetition indicates the importance of the distinction, which is further developed by the barbarian-Scythian pairing. The Scythians were a nomadic people from the Caucasus who were known for their cruelty. The idea is that in Christ ethnic differences of even the most extreme kind lose their importance—a key theme in Colossians. The little attention to the "slave" and "free" distinction, and the omission of the male and female pairing are noteworthy (see 3:18–4:1). The focus is on the ethnic differences.

The concluding formula in 3:11 ("Christ is all and in all") summarizes the theology of the entire letter. It flows from what was said about Christ in the hymn in 1:15-20. It applies what is said about God in 1 Corinthians 15:28 ("so that God may be all in all") to Christ.

Virtues to Be Pursued (3:12-17)

> [12] Put on then, as God's chosen ones, holy and beloved, heartfelt compassion, kindness, humility, gentleness, and patience, [13] bearing with one another and forgiving one another, if one has a grievance against another; as the Lord has forgiven you, so must you also do. [14] And over all these put on love, that is, the bond of perfection. [15] And let the peace of Christ control your hearts, the peace into which you were also called in one body. And be thankful. [16] Let the word of Christ dwell in you richly, as in all wisdom you teach and admonish one another, singing psalms, hymns, and spiritual songs with gratitude in your hearts to God. [17] And whatever you do, in word or in deed, do everything in the name of the Lord Jesus, giving thanks to God the Father through him.

The opening command ("put on then") in 3:12 signals what those who have been raised with Christ (3:1) should do in the present. The command introduces a list of five virtues (the counterpart of the two sets of five vices in 3:5, 8) and is complemented by two participles in 3:13a ("bearing with ... forgiving"). After rooting forgiveness within the community in God's willingness to forgive sins (3:13b), the passage extols love as the "bond" of all the virtues and the way to perfection (3:14). Then come two wishes: "Let the peace of Christ control your hearts" (3:15), and "let the word of Christ dwell in you" (3:16). The final two sentences (3:16-17) move from worship within the community (3:16) to the Pauline idea of everyday life as the setting for Christian worship (3:17).

The command in 3:12 ("put on then") stands in line with the commands in the previous section (3:5, 8, 9) but takes a positive direction. There is probably an allusion back to the baptismal imagery in 3:10 of putting on the "new self." The three descriptions ("God's chosen ones, holy and beloved") assume that God has acted first and that the exalted status of Christians is a consequence of the divine initiative. Just as the preceding lists of vices had five members, so the list of virtues in 3:12 has five members: "heartfelt compassion, kindness, humility, gentleness, and patience." All five virtues refer to life within the Christian community. For other lists of virtues see Galatians 5:22-23 and the Qumran *Community Rule* 4:3-6.

The two participles in 3:13 ("bearing with ... forgiving") continue the series of instructions regarding life within the community. Willingness to forgive others is rooted in God's willingness to forgive those who themselves have experienced the forgiveness of sins in baptism (see Mt 6:14-15; Mk 11:25-26).

As the "bond of perfection," love in 3:14 is compared to an outer garment (like a sweater or coat today) that embraces and holds together all the other virtues. See Romans 13:8-10 and 1 Corinthians 13:1-13 for similar evaluations of the importance of love. The "bond" joins together all the virtues and thus moves the person and community toward "perfection." The image of the "bond" was used by Pythagoreans with regard to friendship and by Plato with regard to the true idea of the right, beautiful, and good.

The "peace of Christ" (3:15) has been made possible through his death and resurrection, and opened up to those who have been baptized in him. The communal dimension of Christ's peace is brought out by the expression "called in one body." The thankfulness demanded at the end of 3:15 probably prepares for the references to communal worship in 3:16.

The "word of Christ" in 3:16 is the gospel, that is, the word about Christ, which is the starting point for all teaching and admonishing. It is impossible to make precise distinctions among "psalms, hymns, and spiritual songs." All three proceed from the Holy Spirit and so are "spiritual." Pliny the Younger (*Epistles* 10.96) described the early Christians at worship as "singing songs to Christ as to a god." For early Christian hymns in the New Testament, see Colossians 1:15-20; Philippians 2:6-11; John 1:1-18; and 1 Timothy 3:16. The final sentence (3:17) broadens the Christian arena of worship to include the whole of life (see Rom 12:1-2). Praise in everyday life is offered to God the Father through Christ.

This passage is especially important for its approach to Christian virtue. For the Christian, virtue is first and foremost a response to being chosen, made holy, and loved by God (3:12a). The five virtues in the list in 3:12b are all predicated elsewhere of God or of Christ: heartfelt com-

122

passion (Rom 12:1; 2 Cor 1:3), kindness (Rom 2:4; 11:2), humility (Phil 2:8), gentleness (2 Cor 10:1), and patience (Rom 2:4; 9:22). Thus the virtues are not so much human creations or achievements as they are opportunities to share in the new life opened up by God through Christ. Thus in urging mutual forgiveness it is appropriate to appeal to God's prior willingness to forgive sinners (3:13b). The centrality of love (3:14) among the virtues gives a simplicity and coherence to the teaching as a whole. The second part of the passage (3:15-17) connects the virtues to life in community (3:15), formal worship (3:16), and worship in everyday life (3:17).

The Household Code (3:18–4:1)

[18] Wives, be subordinate to your husbands, as is proper in the Lord. [19] Husbands, love your wives, and avoid any bitterness toward them. [20] Children, obey your parents in everything, for this is pleasing to the Lord. [21] Fathers, do not provoke your children, so they may not become discouraged.

[22] Slaves, obey your human masters in everything, not only when being watched, as currying favor, but in simplicity of heart, fearing the Lord. [23] Whatever you do, do from the heart, as for the Lord and not for others, [24] knowing that you will receive from the Lord due payment of the inheritance; be slaves of the Lord Christ. [25] For the wrongdoer will receive recompense for the wrong he committed, and there is no partiality. [4:1] Masters, treat your slaves justly and fairly, realizing that you too have a Master in heaven.

In 3:18–4:1 we have the earliest example of a Christian "household code." The text describes the duties and obligations of three pairs of people who constituted the ancient household: wives and husbands (3:18-19), children and fathers (3:20-21), and slaves and masters (3:22–4:1). In each case the writer addresses the social inferior first and the social superior second. The first two units are brief, whereas the instructions to slaves in 3:22-25 are quite extensive.

To the commonly held idea ("as is proper") that wives should be subordinate to their husbands, 3:18 adds the qualification "in the Lord" (= Christ), thus pointing to the one who is superior to the husband and giving relationships within the household a distinctively Christian framework. The husband according to 3:19 is to show affection for his wife and not to take out his anger against her. This text cannot be taken as permitting spousal abuse.

Whereas the command to wives was to "be subordinate," to the children and the slaves it is to "obey" (3:20, 22). In the Decalogue the command is to "honor" one's parents. But there the addressees are adults who must care for their elderly parents. Here the children are young, still being raised by their parents in the household, and therefore needing to show obedience to their parents. The command not to "provoke" one's children in 3:21 is directed to the father as head of the household. Despite his authority, he too has obligations to even the most insignificant members of the household.

Throughout 3:22–4:1 there is a play on the word "lord," which refers to the "master" as well as to Christ the Master (Lord) under whom all earthly masters stand and by whom they will be judged. In the Greek philosophical tradition slaves performed services but were not understood to have duties or obligations in the social sphere.

The negative behavior of slaves is characterized in 3:22 by the terms "being watched" and "currying favor." In both cases the aim is to catch the master's attention and to put on a display for him. A more appropriate attitude consists in sincerity and fear of the Lord (serving the only master who really counts).

The positive ideal for slaves is to work "from the heart" (3:23) and to please the Lord as they work. This echoes the injunction in 3:17 to "do everything in the name of the Lord Jesus." In 3:24 the motif of judgment by Christ the Lord as the definitive assessment of one's faithful service is introduced. Christ is the Master who rewards faithful servants and punishes wrongdoers (3:25). The term "partiality" refers to "accepting someone's person/face" (that is, status) and appears also in Romans 2:11; Ephesians 6:9; and James 2:1. The exhortation in 4:1 for masters to treat their slaves "justly and fairly" is common in ancient discussions of slavery (see Sir 4:30; 7:30-31; 33:31). Here the fair treatment of slaves is given a religious dimension: "realizing that you too have a Master in heaven."

Much of the content of the household code in 3:18–4:1 reflects the cultural assumptions of the Greco-Roman world of the first century, including Jews in Palestine and the Diaspora. The precise literary form, though unusual, became very popular in early Christian circles (Eph 5:22–6:9; 1 Pt 2:18–3:7; 1 Tm 2:8-15; 6:1-2; Ti 2:1-10; Didache 4:9-11; Barnabas 19:5-7; 1 Clement 21:6-9). Whether we are to assume that everyone in the household was a Christian is not clear, since most households at this point in early Christian history would probably have been mixed, with Christian, pagan, and perhaps even Jewish members.

The basic social stance of 3:18–4:1 is conservative. It accepts the social institutions of marriage, family, and slavery as "given" and seeks to guide Christians on how to behave within the social framework. There is no direct attempt at reorganizing society according to other standards; any such attempts from first-century Christians could not have succeeded anyhow.

Nevertheless, there are in 3:18–4:1 subtle modifications of social assumptions. There are mutual responsibilities between husbands and wives, and so there are limits to the husband's control over his wife. Fathers are urged to be sensitive to the feelings of their children. Even the institution of slavery is relativized by the recognition that the ultimate Master is Christ the Lord and that there will be a final judgment by Christ on both slaves and masters.

Two sets of motivations run through the instruction. The first set, rooted in the Greek philosophical tradition, grounds the directives in the good order of society: "as is proper" (3:18), "for this is pleasing" (3:20), and "justly and fairly" (4:1). The second set is more clearly Christian: "in the Lord" (3:18, 20), "fearing the Lord" (3:22), "as for the Lord" (3:23), and "realizing that you too have a Master in heaven" (4:1).

The disproportionate attention given to slaves (3:22–4:1) may reflect a particular debate at Colossae. Perhaps the scenario underlying Paul's letter to Philemon played itself out in other cases. Perhaps slaves who became Christians were insisting on "neither slave nor free" (see 3:11; Gal 3:28). Without overturning or opposing the institution of slavery, the text shows how both slaves and masters are to behave "in the Lord."

Today the more controversial element in 3:18–4:1 concerns the subordination of wives to their husbands. In the modern West at least such language is no longer acceptable. And just as no one (I hope) today would argue for reinstituting human slavery on the basis of 3:22–4:1, so there is no need to defend the subordination of women on the basis of 3:18-19. Social patterns change, and we must acknowledge that the husband-wife relationship is changing too.

This text, however, still conveys Christian wisdom in its insistence that all human relationships and duties take place "in the Lord," that these relationships and duties are mutual or two-sided, and that all social institutions are relativized by the recognition that the ultimate Master is Christ the Lord.

Missionary Prayer and Action (4:2-6)

> [2] Persevere in prayer, being watchful in it with thanksgiving; [3] at the same time, pray for us, too, that God may open a door to us for the word, to speak of the mystery of Christ, for which I am in prison, [4] that I may make it clear, as I must speak. [5] Conduct yourselves wisely toward outsiders, making the most of the opportunity. [6] Let your speech always be gracious, seasoned with salt, so that you know how you should respond to each one.

The final exhortations (4:2-6) resume the style left off in 3:17. The first section (4:2-4) concerns prayer—the Colossians' prayer for their own concerns (4:2) and for the success of Paul's apostolic activities (4:3-4). The second section (4:5-6) concerns how the Colossians should interact with outsiders.

The idea of persistent prayer in 4:2 appears elsewhere in Paul's letters (see Rom 12:12; 1 Thes 5:17). The

127

mention of thanksgiving links these final exhortations back to 3:17. Just as Paul prays for the Colossians persistently (see 1:3, 9), so according to 4:3 they should pray for him. The request for prayers is part of Paul's final comments in Romans 15:30 and Philemon 22 (see also 1 Thes 5:25; 2 Thes 3:1; Eph 6:18). The image of the "door ... for the word" refers primarily to the apostolic opportunities granted to Paul and only secondarily to his release from imprisonment (see 1 Cor 16:9; 2 Cor 2:12). In 1:26-27 (see 2:2) the "mystery of Christ" was defined as the proclamation of the good news of Jesus Christ to the Gentiles. Only at this point (4:3; see also 4:10, 18) are we told that Paul is in prison for the gospel. The verb "make it clear" in 4:4 fits with the idea of the gospel as a mystery being revealed or unveiled (see 1:26-27; 2:2; 4:3).

In 4:5-6 the Colossians are urged to let their encounters with "outsiders" function as a missionary opportunity. It is not clear whether the outsiders were Jews or Gentiles (or both). The Colossians are told to treat outsiders in a gracious manner ("seasoned with salt"), adapted to their sensibilities and needs.

Messages and Greetings (4:7-18)

⁷Tychicus, my beloved brother, trustworthy minister, and fellow slave in the Lord, will tell you all the news of me. ⁸I am sending him to you for this very purpose, so that you may know about us and that he may encourage your hearts, ⁹together with Onesimus, a trustworthy and beloved brother, who is one of you. They will tell you about everything here.

¹⁰Aristarchus, my fellow prisoner, sends you greetings, as does Mark the cousin of Barnabas (concerning

whom you have received instructions; if he comes to you, receive him), and [11] Jesus, who is called Justus, who are of the circumcision; these alone are my co-workers for the kingdom of God, and they have been a comfort to me. [12] Epaphras sends you greetings; he is one of you, a slave of Christ [Jesus], always striving for you in his prayers so that you may be perfect and fully assured in all the will of God. [13] For I can testify that he works very hard for you and for those in Laodicea and those in Hierapolis. [14] Luke the beloved physician sends greetings, as does Demas.

[15] Give greetings to the brothers in Laodicea and to Nympha and to the church in her house. [16] And when this letter is read before you, have it read also in the church of the Laodiceans, and you yourselves read the one from Laodicea. [17] And tell Archippus, "See that you fulfill the ministry that you received in the Lord."

[18] The greeting is in my own hand, Paul's. Remember my chains. Grace be with you.

Messages and greeting are a standard feature of the endings in the Pauline letters. In 4:7-9 Paul says that Tychicus and Onesimus are bringing further information about Paul's situation. Then he gives greetings from those who are with him (4:10-14). Next he greets the Laodiceans (especially Nympha), gives instructions about the public reading and exchange of letters, and leaves instructions for Archippus (4:15-17). The letter ends in 4:18 with Paul's own signature, a plea for remembrance, and a final wish for God's grace.

According to Acts 20:4, Tychicus (4:7) was one of the Asian Christians who accompanied Paul up to Jerusalem with the collection (see also 2 Tm 4:12; Eph 6:21). Here his task is to inform the Colossians about Paul and to encourage them. Onesimus (4:9) is most likely the runaway slave whose conversion to Christianity occasioned Paul's letter to Philemon. The description here suggests that he came from Colossae ("one of you") and that Philemon released him to help Paul in his apostolic activity. Whether he is the Onesimus who became the bishop of Ephesus (see Ignatius, Letter to the Ephesians 1:3; 2:1; 6:2) is not certain.

Aristarchus (4:10) appears also in Philemon 24. According to Acts 19:29; 20:4 he accompanied Paul to Jerusalem; according to Acts 27:2 he went to Rome with Paul. It is difficult to know whether "fellow prisoner" should be taken literally or figuratively (he was in the same city and ministered to Paul). The designation of Mark (4:10) as the cousin (not the nephew) of Barnabas suggests that this is the same figure as in Acts 12–13. If so, there must have been a reconciliation with Paul so that he became Paul's co-worker (see Acts 15:36-41; Phlm 24; 2 Tm 4:11). Since Mark and Jesus Justus (4:11) are identified as Jewish Christians ("of the circumcision"), the others were presumably Gentile Christians.

Epaphras (4:12) in Philemon 23 is called Paul's "fellow prisoner." In 1:7 he is said to have brought the gospel to the Colossians. Here he is identified as "one of you" and given credit for his hard work on behalf of the Colossians, Laodiceans, and Hierapolitans. His goal of having them stand "perfect and fully assured" (4:12) probably alludes to the claims made by the opponents about perfection and to the Christian claim that Christ is the "fullness" (1:19). Luke (4:14) is mentioned also in Philemon 24 and 2 Timothy 4:11 as Paul's co-worker. Only here is he identified as "the beloved physician." Whether he was also the author of the Gospel that bears the name of Luke and the

Acts of the Apostles remains a matter of scholarly dispute. Demas (4:14) is also mentioned in Philemon 24. According to 2 Timothy 4:10, Demas, in love with the present world, deserted Paul and went off to Thessalonica.

According to 4:15, it appears that the Laodicean Christians met at the house of Nympha (see Phlm 2; Rom 16:5; 1 Cor 16:19). The instructions in 4:16 give an idea of how Pauline letters circulated among early Christian communities. What the "one from Laodicea" was and what became of it are not clear. Archippus (4:17) was mentioned in Philemon 2 as "our fellow soldier." What precisely his ministry was can no longer be determined.

The phrase "in my own hand" occurs elsewhere (1 Cor 16:21; 2 Thes 3:17; see also Gal 6:11). The Colossians are urged to be mindful of Paul's sufferings as a prisoner for the gospel (see 1:24). The final prayer for God's grace takes up the greeting of 1:2.

The critical problem encountered in this passage is its relation to the letter to Philemon. Most of the names occur in both letters. The easiest explanation is that Paul wrote both letters about the same time. Those who regard Colossians as pseudepigraphic contend that the writer copied from the letter to Philemon or had access to other sources of information. Since "personal information" was part of the convention of pseudepigraphy, 4:7-18 is not decisive in determining the authorship of Colossians.

Colossians in Christian Life

Imaginative Recreation: As was the case with the letters to Philemon and the Philippians, we can "get into" this text and make it our own by identifying ourselves with its original recipients. Imagine that you are a Gentile Christian who came to Christian faith through the ministry of Epaphras, the co-worker of Paul. Imagine that now some of your Jewish friends are saying that Pauline Christianity is only an inferior kind of Judaism. Imagine that these Jewish friends are promising visions of the heavenly court and participation in the angelic chorus if only you observe the precepts of Judaism and prepare yourself properly to receive these visions.

How wonderful Christian faith was at first! We heard Epaphras telling us about Jesus—a Jew who died a shameful death on the cross some twenty-five years ago. He was put to death by the Romans. But his death had meaning not only for his first followers but also for all the people of the world. You see, Epaphras told us, he did not stay dead. His tomb was found empty, and his followers experienced him as still alive. Epaphras told us that through Jesus' death and resurrection even we non-Jews can be part of the people of God and can expect eternal life with God. How wonderful Christian faith was at first!

Then, however, some of our Jewish friends told us that they had a better way. Their Judaism promised knowledge about the structure of the universe and entry into the heavenly court where the angels praise God. All we need to do is to prepare ourselves properly by asceticism and fasting, getting ourselves into the proper mood. They told us that we could go beyond Christianity.

Then came this letter from Paul, or at least in Paul's name. Paul was the teacher of Epaphras. That letter set us straight again. It told us that Christ is the Wisdom of God and that there is no going beyond Christianity. There is no hidden wisdom that has not been revealed in Christ. Christ is all and in all.

The letter also challenged us to live according to our new life in Christ, according to our baptismal promises. It told us to avoid our old vices and to pursue virtue, in a spirit of love. It told us to love and respect the members of our familes and household "in the Lord."

We do not need more than we have already been given in the gospel preached by Epaphras. What we do need is to recognize how wonderful Christian life is when we let ourselves be guided by Christ the Wisdom of God and when we act in ways that befit those who have died with Christ and have been raised with him.

Points for Meditation: The hymn about Christ as the Wisdom of God is the most important part of the letter to the Colossians for understanding the significance of Christ. It portrays Jesus as the Wisdom of God and as the head of the body (the Church). It celebrates Christ as the firstborn from the dead and through his death the agent of reconciliation of the whole universe to God. As the exposition shows, the hymn in 1:15-20 provides the main text for the whole letter and illustrates how faith in Christ permeates and shapes Christian life.

The Church is identified as the body, with Christ as its head (see 1:18, 24). Thus the Church is more than local congregations (the church at Colossae, or at Ephesus, or at Rome). It is not only world-wide but even cosmic in its extent. It receives guidance and direction from Christ as its head. It is the place where the risen Christ here and now realizes his lordship.

Through Christ's death and resurrection, membership in God's people is open to all, regardless of ethnic background. Indeed, the message of Colossians is that "Christ is all and in all" (3:11). The mystery of Christ is not only for Jews but also for Gentiles (see 1:27). This was (and is) the gospel proclaimed by Paul as apostle to the Gentiles.

Colossians is perhaps most important for its teachings about Christian life. It corrects the error of those who search for wisdom by esoteric means. It insists that God's true wisdom has been revealed in Christ Jesus. If we want to know who God is and what God wants for us and from us, we need only look to Christ as the Wisdom of God. Christ as the firstborn of all creation and the firstborn of the dead is the Lord over everything, including the Christian's daily life.

Through baptism the Christian shares in Jesus' life, death, and resurrection. This incorporation into Christ must express itself in appropriate actions. Thus participation in the Christ-event serves as the starting point for Christian ethics (see 2:20–3:4).

In many respects the life of the good Christian according to Colossians looked much like that of other people of good will in the first century. There were vices to be avoided (see 3:5, 8) and virtues to be pursued (see 3:12-13), with love as the "bond of perfection" (3:14). The ideal of the Christian household (see 3:18–4:1) was orderliness and mutual respect, "as it proper in the Lord" (3:18). The explicitly Christian motivations place what was common ethical teaching in the framework of faith and love.

People of our time find the household code (3:18–4:1) especially problematic, since it assumes the existence of slavery and promotes the subordination of wives to husbands. While those assumptions seemed acceptable to people in the first century, they are not acceptable to most people today. The challenge posed by such texts is to discern what belonged to the culture of the past (the patriarchal household and slavery) and to focus on the positive and lasting values (mutual respect and dealing with one another "in the Lord").

As was the case with Philemon and Philippians, Colossians reminds us that the Pauline mission was not a one-man show but rather the work of a pastoral team that developed a network of communication. Without his co-workers and friends, Paul could not have accomplished what he did in spreading the good news of Jesus Christ. If Colossians was composed by an admirer of Paul around A.D. 80, we can see how his teachings were received and adapted to meet the new challenges that faced the Pauline churches—another indication of the collaborative nature of the Pauline mission.

Prayer: O God the Father of our Lord Jesus Christ, we give you thanks and praise for Christ Jesus, your perfect Wisdom, first in creation and first in redemption. We thank you for our new life in Christ through faith and baptism in his name. We thank you for those who have brought us to Christ faith and sustained us in it.

Protect us from the illusion that we can save ourselves through pious practices and rituals alone. Help us to see how we can show forth in our everyday lives the wisdom and new life that we have in Christ Jesus. Help us to put away the vices proper to the "old self" and to put on the virtues proper to the "new self." Help us to respect and love those of our family and indeed all those whom we encounter. We make this prayer through Christ, the Wisdom of God, who is all and in all. Amen.

For Further Study

Barrett, C. K. *Paul. An Introduction to His Thought* (Louisville: Westminster/Knox, 1994).

Barth, M. and H. Blanke. *Colossians* (New York: Doubleday, 1994).

Becker, J. *Paul. Apostle to the Gentiles* (Louisville: Westminster/Knox, 1994).

Dunn, J.D.G. *The Epistles to the Colossians and to Philemon* (Grand Rapids: Eerdmans, 1996).

Fitzmyer, J. A. *Paul and His Theology* (Englewood Cliffs, NJ: Prentice-Hall, 1989).

Lohse, E. *Colossians and Philemon* (Philadelphia: Fortress, 1971).

Meeks, W. *The First Urban Christians. The Social World of the Apostle Paul* (New Haven: Yale University Press, 1983).

Murphy-O'Connor, J. *Paul. A Critical Life* (Oxford: Claredon Press, 1996).

_____. *Paul the Letter-Writer* (Collegeville: Liturgical Press, 1995).

O'Brien, P. T. *Colossians. Philemon* (Waco, TX: Word, 1982).

_____. *The Epistle to the Philippians* (Grand Rapids: Eerdmans, 1991).

Petersen, N. R. *Rediscovering Paul. Philemon and the Sociology of Paul's Narrative World* (Philadelphia: Fortress, 1985).

Pokorny, P. *Colossians* (Peabody, MA: Hendrickson, 1991).

Rapske, B. *Paul in Roman Custody* (Grand Rapids: Eerdmans, 1994).

Schweizer, E. *The Letter to the Colossians. A Commentary* (Minneapolis: Augsburg, 1982).

Silva, M. *Philippians* (Grand Rapids: Baker, 1992).

Wansink, C.S. *Chained in Christ. The Experience and Rhetoric of Paul's Imprisonments* (Sheffield: Sheffield Academic Press, 1996).